Male-Dominated
Stories of a Woman in Law Enforcement

By Nenia Corcoran

ISBN-13: **979-8-9850375-1-7**

Cover design by Annemieke Beemster Leverenz

*Dedicated to all the men
I've worked with who weren't sexist,
but still managed to be pretty damn sexist.*

A Note From The Author

The stories and situations contained in these pages are real. These are my actual experiences from my point of view.

While I chose not to use names while telling these stories, I didn't attempt to disguise the individuals I wrote about. They will likely recognize themselves within these stories, and I'm sure they will disagree with my truth. No one ever sees eye to eye on a truth that involves something controversial, like sexism.

I'm sure the unnamed individuals will argue that I'm blowing these stories out of proportion or that I misunderstood the situation. Some of them will deny their involvement altogether and claim I'm simply making things up. They will act outraged at the implication they might be sexist, or at the very least, did or said something sexist.

They'll stomp their feet, pound their fists, and claim that they've never done a sexist thing in their whole lives and that this is precisely why women don't belong in law enforcement. I can already hear the echoes of whiny shrieks saying, "women are just too sensitive!"

In many ways, that reaction is exactly why I need to tell these stories. The intent of this book is not to point fingers at the specific individuals I happened to interact with throughout my career, but there's no way to have this larger conversation about the issues in law enforcement without sharing my specific experiences.

In these pages, I don't speak for all women in law enforcement. I don't speak for most women in law enforcement. I can quite literally only speak for one woman, and that's me. I can tell you the things I personally experienced, how they made me feel, and the changes I would like to see for the future generations of police officers, but that's it.

I am just one woman who wore a badge for ten years in the State of New Hampshire.

There might be women in law enforcement who never dealt with any of the scenarios. I know some women have dealt with situations far worse than I ever experienced.

Generations of women before me fought just to get to this point. But there's more work to be done and more to change.

I've realized that nothing has been gained by NOT telling these stories, so maybe there's some benefit in finally sharing them. For the record, I don't know everything there is to know. I'm not an expert, and I will never claim to be. I don't have a degree in gender studies, and while I proudly identify as a feminist, I won't pretend like gender norms and stereotypes do not frequently influence me. I don't know how to fix the problem. I don't have all the answers. But I do know that not talking about the problem isn't solving anything.

For a long time, I quietly tucked these stories away. I packaged them into little boxes in the back of my mind and told myself they didn't matter. I told myself my career was more important than "small injustices." I convinced myself there was no point in focusing on things I couldn't change.

Maybe I can't change things by telling these stories. After all, I'm just one woman yelling into the void. But I'll be damned if I can't say I at least tried.

The point of telling these stories is not to call out the individuals involved, though they might deserve it. The point of this book is to call out the culture.

But we can't change the culture without changing the individuals...

CHAPTER 1

THE HISTORY

On the first day of the police academy, we learned about Sir Robert Peel. Peel is credited with being the father of modern law enforcement.

In 1829, Peel established uniform patrol officers to protect the streets of London, creating the military-like organization known as the London Metropolitan Police Department. Peel focused on the quality of the men he hired to be officers to establish credibility and provided them with appropriate training to make them better at their jobs.

Peel introduced uniforms and assigned badge numbers to officers to increase accountability. His officers were required to wear their uniforms at all times, work long hours, and seldom had time off. He also required officers to be at least 5'7 and under the age of thirty-five. They were also, shockingly, all men.

While policing looks entirely different today than it did in 1829, Peel's Principles of Policing are still regarded as the cornerstones of policing. At their core, these principles recognize that the role of the police is to prevent crime. To do this, the public must trust and support the police. Today, you might hear this referred to as Community Policing.

Community policing is the current gold standard for American police departments. While the concept is often touted as a revolutionary idea, the reality is Sir Robert Peel already had it all figured out way back when he first established his Bobbies.

While Peel and his police principles are well documented in the history of police work, the history of women police officers is a bit sketchier. Depending on where you look, you might see different results for who the first woman police officer was and when she was sworn in.

Maria Owens and Lola Baldwin are common names you might hear, having worked for

Chicago PD and Portland PD, respectively, as early as 1891. This might make it seem like women made an early start in the world of policing, but these women were not doing the same jobs as their male coworkers.

These women were first hired as jail matrons or tasked with dealing with children and other women. In some cases, these women were given the title patrolman, but their duties more closely resembled social work than policing.

As policing developed in the United States, women took support roles within the departments, like administrative assistants and dispatchers.

In 1968, Indianapolis became the first police department to assign a patrol vehicle to two women, Elizabeth Robinson and Betty Blankenship. Despite this momentous achievement, Robinson and Blankenship were not provided any of the training their male coworkers received and were essentially left to fend for themselves. Their uniform consisted of a skirt and high heels. They had to carry their handguns in purses instead of on a gun belt. They were hardly taken seriously.

The passing of Title VII of the Civil Rights Act in 1972 outlawed gender discrimination, increasing women's opportunities within law enforcement agencies. Women have come a long way from the skirts and purses of Robinson and Blankenship's day, but challenges still exist for women seeking careers in this male-dominated field. Just because discrimination is illegal doesn't mean it doesn't happen.

The number of women making up the law enforcement community has hovered in the area of 15% for years. The term male-dominated is clearly an accurate description of the profession. But it's more than just the ratio of men to women. Law enforcement is controlled by male ideas, male egos, and male stereotypes.

It's not that women *can't* succeed in law enforcement. We've proven ourselves more than capable of every possible position within the profession. We're able to rise through the ranks and hold specialty positions. We're able to have successful careers. We can do the job, but not without struggle and sacrifice. Not without giving in to certain attitudes and accepting certain truths.

Women in law enforcement have to play by different rules than men. To succeed, we have to fit into the box our male coworkers have created for us. This profession is not only dominated physically by men, but it's dominated by male voices unwilling to make room for anyone else.

CHAPTER 2

THE UNWRITTEN RULES

When I first started thinking about writing this book, I mentioned it to a friend of mine.

"You can't write those stories," he said, looking absolutely appalled. "It will make law enforcement look sexist."

I stared at him, trying to decide if he was joking. I quickly realized he was not.

"Those are just things that happened to you," he argued, "it's not like they happen to everyone."

"Right. They're things that happened to me because I'm a woman." I tried speaking a little slower than normal, so my friend could keep up.

"I know, but if you write about them like that, it'll make it all sound sexist."

"Right," I said, "because it is sexist."

He shook his head and threw up his hands.

"Not everything that happens is because of sexism!"

Believe it or not, this was not the first time I had met opposition regarding whether my experiences with sexism constituted as "actual" sexism. In my experience, men like to be the judge of what sexism is, and their definition is usually pretty lax.

It's an interesting situation, to be a female in a male-dominated field.

As I'll share in these chapters, I spent a lot of my career ignoring sexist behaviors. Being able to overlook everyday sexism was essentially a necessary job skill. I got so good at it that I could have listed it on my resume.

However, it never ceased to amaze me that if I did choose to speak out against a particularly blatant act of sexism or sexual harassment, how quickly it would get spun back around on me.

"Here we go again, playing the 'girl card,'" or

"Not everything is sexist. Lighten up."

No matter how infrequently I brought the topic up, my male coworkers would act as if I harped on the subject constantly. They would act exasperated at the mere mention of sexism.

On the rare occasion, I tried to draw attention to something specific, the men around me would act personally offended, behaving as if I was always falsely accusing them. The audacity of me to think them capable of sexism! Their reactions were so ridiculous, they were almost comical.

The truth is, it's an unwritten rule that you can't really complain about sexism or sexual harassment in the law enforcement world.

Of course, legally, you can.

Legally, filing a complaint can't have any repercussions or negative results. Legally, you should be able to work in an environment free from sexism and sexual harassment and feel entirely comfortable reporting such behaviors to your supervisor or your human resources department. Legally, you are entitled to work in a hostility-free environment.

But realistically, in the law enforcement world, making a sexist or sexual harassment complaint would be the end of your career.

Everyone knows (though no one would ever actually say it) that if you are a woman and you make a complaint, you're out.

No one would ever trust you again. No one would have your back. You'd be treated like a pariah.

You wouldn't be able to leave your department and go to work anywhere else because the fact that you made the complaint would follow you. You'd have a reputation. You'd be a chief's worst nightmare. You'd be an 'issue waiting to happen,' considered too sensitive to be doing this job in a male-dominated field. You wouldn't "have what it takes." Your law enforcement career would be over.

Instead of calling it out or reporting it, the women of law enforcement and other male-dominated fields have had to adapt. The adaptation is developing the ability to simply ignore sexual harassment and sexism. Essentially, we have no choice. There's no other way to have a successful career.

I've played by the unwritten rules of law enforcement for ten years. I've put up with a decade of this bullshit. I've quietly ignored nearly 3,650 days' worth of sexism and sexual harassment.

But I don't feel like being quiet anymore.

I'm going to break the rules.

I'm going to share my stories. I'm going to talk about the times I experienced sexism, sexual harassment, and discrimination. I'm going to tell the stories without sugarcoating them or laughing off the bad parts. I'm going to call it all out.

These are my experiences. These are the true stories, from my point of view, of what it was like to be a woman in law enforcement in a small community. I'm fully aware that not everyone will like the fact that I'm telling these stories. Some people might even be angry that I'm speaking out about them.

But that's part of the problem, isn't it?

Women keep pretending everything is okay and laughing off these behaviors so that we'll fit in. That just reinforces the male-dominated culture.

By ignoring sexism and sexual harassment, we've been allowing the men to keep forcing us into the position of needing to ignore it.

It took me ten years, but I finally figured out I'm not one of the guys.

I'm a woman.

And I'm not going to be silent anymore.

CHAPTER 3
DON'T GET PREGNANT

In 2012, I sat in the corner office across from the Chief of Police of a small town in New Hampshire. On the desk in front of me was a letter on official letterhead formally offering me a conditional position as a police officer.

I was 22 years old. I was wearing a grey pantsuit my mother had found in Marshalls that was a strange cross between being too girlish and overly professional. I was wearing heels because they made me over six feet tall, and I felt like that made me intimidating. I was wearing my hair half up and half down because I couldn't decide whether it was worse to wear it down and look cute or up and look too severe.

I was young, naive, and clueless. Not just about police work but also about life. I had absolutely no idea what signing my name on that offer letter would lead to. I had no idea what I was doing or what I was getting myself into.

Law enforcement is not just a job. It's a career, a lifestyle, and a calling. It's not the type of job where going through the motions is enough to get you by. It becomes who you are. It defines you, your life, and your future. I knew this, but at the same time, I also had no idea.

After officially accepting my conditional offer, the Police Chief offered me the first formal advice I would get regarding the rest of my police career.

"Don't get pregnant," he said, steepling his fingers on his desk. "Definitely not before or during the academy."

I smiled nervously.

I had no idea how to respond to this statement. It didn't seem to be a joke. The chief was staring at me, straight-faced and serious.

I didn't have any immediate plans to get pregnant. I didn't even have any long-term plans to get pregnant. But it seemed strange to share that with a man I had met for the first time in the hallway outside his office ten minutes earlier. A man who was technically now my boss.

"You can retire at forty-five," he said. "That's really not too late to consider waiting to get pregnant until then, you know. Retire and then start a family."

This time I laughed. It wasn't the appropriate response, but I didn't have any idea what the appropriate response was. I was probably supposed to nod or offer some sort of acknowledgment that I understood, but I didn't.

I've always been a nervous laugher. Put me in an uncomfortable situation, and it's only a matter of time before I start giggling. In this particularly strange situation, sitting across from the man who had just hired me to join his police force and then instructed me not to get pregnant, I laughed.

When I told this story about the chief later, years after his death, others laughed too.

"That sounds like something the chief would do," people said. "He was that type of guy."

I accepted this as an explanation. After all, I knew a lot of 'those types of guys.'

Those types of guys who couldn't help but say inappropriate things.
Those types of guys who were from that time where that kind of thing was the norm.

Those types of guys who just couldn't quite filter themselves.

Those types of guys.

You know the type, right?

I met a lot of "those types of guys" in my line of work. Police work, after all, is a male-dominated profession.

A man's world.

A boy's club.

I was constantly reminded of this during the decade I spent donning a uniform. That very first meeting with the Chief of Police all those years ago was really just the beginning. Not just the beginning of my career but the beginning of the nearly constant sexual harassment and sexism I would face under the guise of my job being male-dominated.

Between the day I was hired and the day I left, I sat for a number of different oral-board interviews for various hiring and promotional processes. In each and every one of them, someone asked what I planned to do if I got pregnant.

I was asked this question by Police Chiefs, Selectmen, and Town Administrators.

Over the course of my ten-year career, I was probably asked this question more than two dozen times while attempting to advance my career.

Each time it was brought up, my mind returned to the corner office where the Chief first advised me not to get pregnant. I'd remember my nervous laughter and the serious look on the Chief's face.

Then I would think, "where do these assholes get the balls to ask me that?"

The term male-dominated refers to a lot more than just the ratio of men and women in the field. It has nothing to do with how many of them there are, and everything to do with how they act.

CHAPTER 4
PATROLMEN

We rarely get the chance to look in the mirror and experience pure, overwhelming pride in who we are.

I'll never forget the day I stood in front of the mirror in the women's locker room wearing my uniform for the first time. Seeing that silver badge over my heart filled me with feelings, I can't exactly find words for. It was a feeling I'd never experienced before and have never experienced since. The closest words I can find in the English language to describe it are pride, joy, nerves, excitement, and fear, but all mixed together in an overwhelming tsunami of emotion.

It was different than the feeling of accomplishment. This moment was only a baby step in my journey to becoming a certified police officer. I still had months of training ahead of me before that "I did it!" moment would come.

Staring in that mirror for the first time was more of a personal awakening. It was the first time I allowed myself to believe I had what it takes to become something bigger than myself. It was a powerful, almost spiritual moment.

But, there was something not quite right with what I saw in the reflection of that dirty locker room mirror, and even then, I knew it. I could feel it.

The very first thing they teach you about being a police officer is command presence. The way you look when you walk into a scene plays an essential role in the amount of respect you receive.

It's an attitude, a confidence that can be learned but not necessarily taught. It's a way of carrying yourself that portrays confidence and capableness. It's the look that says, "I know what I'm doing, and I've got this."

The officer's appearance when they arrive on the scene is critical in determining how every second that follows during a call will play out.

When the officer steps out of their patrol car, do they look like someone you respect?

Do they look like they know how to do their job?

This is why there's so much debate on whether police officers should have tattoos and beards and how long their hair can be. Does having an arm full of colored ink make them seem unprofessional? Does having a beard make them look lazy? These are the questions thrown around again and again in the endless debates around uniform regulations.

The uniform is a key part to that overall look. The uniform itself provides a certain amount of authority. This is, after all, the reason uniforms are worn. Uniforms give a sense of legitimacy, reassurance, and recognition, which is why the police, the military, and even chain companies, still wear them. The uniform itself means something, all on its own.

But the message the uniform portrays differs based on how it looks. In order to be taken seriously, it must be put together, clean, polished, and professional. A sloppy uniform indicates a sloppy officer. Sloppy officers aren't seen as capable. When officers aren't seen as capable, they're in danger.

Early in my career, I was told that a study had been done with several criminals who had attacked and murdered police officers. Supposedly, many, if not all, of these criminals stated that they decided they could attack the officer based on what the officer looked like when he arrived on scene. Apparently, these murderers stressed that if an officer looked like shit in the uniform, they took that as a sign they could easily win the attack and get away.

Maybe that was just a scare tactic some academy cadre used to justify why we needed to iron creases into our tee-shirts, but I never forgot it. That, plus my own experiences, led me to conclude that more than half of police work is showing up and looking the part.

But standing in the women's locker room, I didn't know all this yet. I hadn't been formally taught the importance of how I looked yet.

But still, some sort of learned societal understanding nagged at the back of my mind. I knew something wasn't right.

I was undeniably proud. But I knew, deep down, the girl looking back at me didn't look the part. The girl I was looking at was nervous and young. You could see that even under the eagerness and determination she was trying to force to the surface. She wasn't confident, but hopefully, that would come with time.

It was more than that, though. She didn't look put together and polished, despite the badge. There was something just not right about her uniform.

For one thing, it was at least two sizes too large.

The Lieutenant in charge of outfitting me with a uniform made a particular comment while digging through the storage room of used uniforms during my first week.

"Uniforms aren't supposed to be sexy."

He then handed me several extra-large-size shirts. I had always been considered tall, but I had never been described as large. You'd probably have described me as petite if I had been shorter.

I had a thin frame and long, bony limbs, despite how hard I worked to put muscle on them. I was, at best, a men's small.

Needless to say, nothing about my uniform fit correctly. My short sleeves hung down to my forearms. There was so much excess fabric on the sides of my shirt that I had to fold it over itself to tuck it into my pants. The bottoms of the breast pockets were touching the top of my duty belt, and the tails of my shirt reached my knees. The pants bunched together in the front, where I had to pull my belt tight in order to keep them on. It squished the belt loops together, so they were nearly all touching. The extra fabric bubbled out from under the equipment on my belt.

I didn't have to worry about my uniform looking 'too sexy.' On the contrary, it looked dumpy. I looked like a small child trying on my father's clothes, a little girl playing dress-up on Halloween. The only thing that fit me were the boots. Shiny, black Corcoran jump boots stood out from under the frayed hem of my hand-me-down pants that were somehow both too big and too short at the same time.

I had also been provided a hand-me-down vest. The vest intended to save my life in the worst-case scenario was too small, having belonged to someone else long before my time. It was too short to protect my vital organs and rode too high on my neck to be comfortable. It always felt like it was choking me, and I developed the habit of pulling it down with my non-dominate hand while driving or talking to witnesses. The Velcro had long ago given out, so I had to use safety pins to keep it strapped around me.

I was never physically comfortable in my uniform, nor did I feel mentally comfortable in it. I knew I didn't look like my coworkers, whose uniforms lay flat and tight against their vests, only bubbling where some had gained weight since the last time they'd been fitted.

But I had no idea this wasn't how new employees were typically outfitted for their uniforms. There were no measurements taken or alternate sizes offered. I was handed equipment, and I didn't ask questions. I wore what I was given as proudly as I could.

It wasn't unusual for people to comment on my uniform. Other officers would wonder aloud why they didn't get me smaller shirts. People on the streets would joke about the potential that I was not actually a police officer but just someone who had stumbled across a uniform in a dumpster and decided to try it on. People would laugh and say it must be "bring your daughter to work day, " implying that whatever male officer I was with could be my father. It became an ongoing, running joke, and I was always the butt of it.

Eventually, long after I had attended the academy and finished my training, making me a permanent member of the department, I made a request to the same lieutenant for new uniform shirts. I was hoping he'd order a size small for me, as that seemed to be the size I actually needed. My request was denied. The lieutenant felt nothing was wrong with my uniform and found no reason to replace my "practically new" shirts.

It wasn't until several years later, when the department changed to a new style of uniform, that I was finally correctly measured for shirts, pants, and a new vest. The representative from the uniform company asked me if I had recently lost weight. He stared at me in confusion when I told him 'no.' The uniform sizes he ordered for me were very different from those I had been wearing since my first day.

But the way my uniform looked wasn't the only equipment issue I ran into in the early days of my career. The badge that adorned my chest, the most critical aspect of my appearance, quickly became another point of contention.

When I was hired, the department members were wearing badges that read 'Patrolman' in black letters above the town seal on the shiny shield.

The term patrolman dates back to the earliest forms of policing. It combines the action of patrolling with the word man, making it a noun. This is relatively common in the English language. Many professions used similar methods of creating titles for those in their fields.

Postman, fireman, fisherman, barman, salesman...you get the point.

The word patrolman didn't bother me any more than the words human or woman. While I recognize the patriarchal significance of using 'man' within all these words, it's a job title at the end of the day. And it was my job title. I took pride in it.

I wasn't offended by being labeled a patrolman. The term is steeped in history, referencing back to Sir Robert Peel and his original principles of policing. It's also the same term that adorns my grandfather's badge from his days as a Boston Motorcycle

Officer, which in many ways made me even more partial to the term.

(Not to mention, I think the term patrolwoman or patrolperson sounds ridiculous).

I was perfectly happy with the badge I was initially handed in September of 2012 when I was sworn in as a member of the department.

But no one asked me my opinion.

Nor did anyone seem to care about it.

A few days after I was handed the badge with the word Patrolman embossed across it, that badge was taken away from me. I was then given a new badge adorned with the politically correct and gender-neutral term 'Officer.'

I was told I needed to wear the gender-neutral badge as it wasn't offensive to a woman.

Just like I had no issue with the term patrolman, I have no issue with the term officer. The issue with the badge was that I was the only one being forced to wear it. No one else in the department was being asked to change to the gender-neutral badge.

I tried to argue that this poor attempt at equality actually had the opposite effect. It singled me out by forcing me to wear a badge that was different from the rest of the department. The men were all Patrolmen, but I was something different. The badge segregated me instead of including me.

My point fell on very deaf ears.

I was told that I couldn't wear the badge that labeled me a patrolman because I was a woman. I was told that the Officer badge was not offensive and was, therefore, better for me. I was told the Officer badge wasn't sexist, and that should apparently make me happy.

But it didn't make me happy. The fact that I was being told what should and shouldn't offend me felt backward.

As time went on, badges throughout the department were slowly changed out until very few Patrolmen badges still existed. Those hanging on to them were doing so more out of nostalgia than anything else. I was no longer the only one wearing the gender-neutral term, so it eventually became a non-issue.

But it was still frustrating that I couldn't make anyone understand that the sexism had nothing to do with what I was actually referred to as. Patrolman, officer, cop; the specific terminology didn't matter. I just wanted to be called whatever everyone else was being called. I didn't want to be different, and I shouldn't have been forced to be different because of my gender.

At the end of the day, that's what all of this is about. I wasn't looking for special treatment. I wasn't looking for a special badge.

I just wanted to be treated the same as everyone else around me.

CHAPTER 5
THICK SKIN

My first few months as a police officer were a complete blur. There were names to remember, streets to learn, codes to memorize. I was constantly being quizzed or questioned. What would you do in this scenario? How would you handle someone who said this?

Learning to be a police officer is like being dropped into a foreign country with an elementary school understanding of the native language. It's stressful and overwhelming for anyone, but there was an added layer of pressure for me.

I wasn't just trying to learn the job. I also had to learn how to be "one of the guys."

I knew going into the job that I would constantly work twice as hard as those around me to prove myself. I understood that I would be underestimated. I knew I would be seen as weaker and less capable. I had come to terms with these things and was ready to work to combat them. I knew I could prove myself strong and capable. I was sure that I could defy expectations.

I was spending hours in the gym to ensure I was as strong as physically possible. I was studying policies, laws, and procedures. I spent all my free time working to make myself stronger, faster, smarter, and more than just capable. I thought those were the important qualities that would help me fit in with my new coworkers.

I didn't realize that most of those things took a back seat to the real issue. Sure, those areas were important, and if I had failed in any of them, someone would certainly have been quick to point it out. But what seemed to concern my coworkers most of all was whether I had the right "personality" for the environment.

The first time this was mentioned to me, I assumed personality was regarding the mildly dark sense of humor that nearly all first responders seem to possess. While some might call it crass, it's truly a defense mechanism. Being able to find something to laugh about in the absolute worst situations is a way to take some of the horrors out of the absolutely awful things first responders are continuously exposed to.

It takes a certain mentality to see the absolute worst of humanity and still believe that there are good things possible in the world. Finding things worth smiling about after a crisis takes a dark sense of humor.

I knew this was part of the job. I understood that seeing the dark side of life was a necessary evil of police work. I had prepared myself for that, though there would always be moments that still managed to be worse than anything I ever imagined. So when having a thick skin was first mentioned in passing almost immediately after I was hired, I assumed this was what was being referred to.

Shortly after I started my field training, I realized that the 'thick skin' my colleagues were all hoping I had went a little bit deeper than just the ability to laugh in the face of death and destruction.

A Field Training Officer (FTO) is one of the most important aspects of a police officer's development. The FTO is your mentor as you transition into the world of law enforcement. The FTO's job is not only to teach you the fundamentals of the job but also to keep you safe while you learn.

A new police officer usually starts by acting as the FTO's shadow. This allows the new officer to watch everything their FTO does and absorb how they do things without the pressure of making any decisions. It allows the new officer and the FTO to talk through the why's and ask questions without any negative consequences.

As an officer progresses through training, the FTO becomes the new officer's shadow. The officer starts handling situations themselves, but the FTO is there, watching and helping. They guide the new officer when necessary and are ready to step in if needed. The FTO protects the officer while the officer learns to protect themself.

Eventually, the FTO decides whether an officer is ready to begin working alone. They judge whether the officer has the abilities to do the job, make decisions and keep themself and the people around them alive. They ultimately decide whether or not the officer is going to make the cut as a cop.

Being with an FTO is both comforting and nerve-wracking. On the one hand, the FTO is like a safety net. If anything goes wrong, the FTO is there to help sort it out. It's like knowing someone's got your back and will prevent you from falling flat on your face. There's some security in that.

But on the flip side, the FTO is constantly watching and assessing, essentially just waiting for you to make mistakes they can jump on. They can be hard on you; they need to be hard on you. They are critiquing everything, from how you drive to how you stand.

It can be relentless, overwhelming, and draining. But it's a crucial part of the training. The FTO is a significant and influential person in a young police officer's career.

I consider myself truly privileged to have had some incredible training officer's during my early days on the job. Many of the lessons I learned in my first few months as an officer stuck with me through my entire time in uniform. There are specific lessons that, even a decade later, I can still clearly recall as if they just happened yesterday.

Some of those lessons helped me advance my career. Others helped me succeed in specific situations. I'd even credit one or two of them with keeping me alive.

While I learned many lessons from my training officers that I've never forgotten, one has always stood out to me. This lesson didn't help me succeed or grow or become a better officer. This lesson instilled something else altogether in my head, which infiltrated almost every aspect of the rest of my time in law enforcement.

I had a tremendous amount of respect for this training officer, and despite this conversation, I still highly respect him. He is not only good at his job but also a good teacher. He was invested in training me. He pushed me to better myself, unlike the other training officers. He constantly presented me with scenarios that forced me to think outside the box. He asked hard questions and forced me to consider unfavorable outcomes. He encouraged me to talk through my logic and always talked through his, whether it differed from mine or not.

In addition to having the utmost respect for this officer, I trusted him. He was easy to talk to, and even in our idle conversations, I often found tidbits of information I could hold on to. Some were more obvious than others, but there was always something to learn from him. I enjoyed his stories and anecdotes about the town. He was the only officer that could boast he grew up in the town we worked in. It gave him an advantage that no one else on the police force had.

He started this particular conversation by mentioning that it took a certain type of person to be a police officer. He said there was a specific personality type, and some people possessed it, others didn't. He explained that this personality type was one of those things that simply couldn't be taught. You either had it, or you didn't, and it would make or break your future.

Again, I assumed he was talking about that slightly dark sense of humor. I agreed that it didn't seem like something that could be taught. But as the conversation progressed, I realized he was talking about a different personality trait altogether.

"You have to have thick skin," he said. "The types of things guys say around the station, you have to be able to let them roll off your back. If you don't have thick skin, you're not going to fit in in law enforcement."

It turns out that the types of things guys say around the station are the types of things the Human Resource department's do lectures on. Dark humor is the least of anyone's concerns. In the world of law enforcement, skin apparently has to be thick to ignore the sexism and sexual harassment.

At the time, I took what my FTO said to heart. Not only because I respected him, but because what he'd said made sense in a way. I understood this was a man's world. I realized it was male-dominated. I thought my FTO was providing me with valuable insight on how to infiltrate that world.

I took what he said that day to mean that to fit in, I needed to become "one of the guys." That meant hiding everything about myself that was feminine, including my reaction toward sexism and sexual harassment.

I wanted to prove I had thick skin. I wanted to fit in and belong to my new blue family. I didn't want to be outcasted. I took the advice my FTO had given me as a gift. He wanted me to succeed, and he was showing me how best to do it.

I quickly adapted to my new reality. I changed how I dressed, opting for loose tee shirts and cargo pants so as not to draw too much attention to the fact that I was a woman. It's not that I had a whole lot to hide, I'm not exactly well-endowed, but I didn't want to be accused of attempting to dress "sexy." I'd already learned from my uniform situation that looking sexy was seen as a negative quality in female officers.

I hid feminine hobbies from my coworkers, like my love for musical theater. I flaunted the more masculine things I enjoyed, like shooting guns and playing sports. I'd had a tomboy side ever since I was a child, so this didn't necessarily feel like acting. I was just forcing one part of my personality to take the lead.

I'd always had an affinity for swear words, so it was easy to talk tough. I had the talk down, so I just needed to fake walking the walk. I did what I thought I needed to do for the guys to accept me as one of their own.

Unfortunately, I quickly learned that being one of the guys often meant sacrificing my boundaries and accepting sexist comments and sexual harassment nearly daily. The belief that I couldn't speak out or put a stop to this type of behavior without betraying my position among my coworkers followed me throughout my entire career.

I believed that to keep from disrupting the status quo of our department, I had to make my coworkers feel comfortable to "be themselves" around me. I didn't want them to treat me differently because I was a woman or be afraid they couldn't speak openly around me. I thought I had to prove to them that I had the thick skin that was needed to be a police officer. I was constantly trying to show them I was one of them. To do so, I had to sacrifice my own comfort, but it seemed like a small price to pay to be accepted.

A lot of people don't realize that sexual harassment is more than copping a feel as a coworker walks by. Sexual harassment is defined as actions and behaviors that create a hostile working environment, including any unwanted verbal or physical sexual behavior. It can range from comments about a person's clothing, anatomy, or looks, to very serious acts that could also qualify as sexual assault or rape.

The problem with sexual harassment is that to stop it, you have to admit that it's bothering you. You have to be willing to speak out and say that the comments or actions are unwanted. You have to admit you don't have thick enough skin.

I was never able to bring myself to make those admissions. I didn't want to be seen as too sensitive. I didn't want to be cast out of the good graces of the guys or seen as an issue. I was afraid of the consequences.

Legally, there can be no consequences or repercussions against someone who makes a sexual harassment complaint. Legally, everything would have been fine if I had decided to stand up to the sexual harassment I witnessed and experienced. But that's horseshit, and we all know it. As soon as I even started in the direction of a complaint, everything would have changed. No, not legally, of course, but the future of my career would be altered beyond repair.

Does that excuse why I ignored and even participated in sexist and harassing behavior? Of course not. There's no excuse I can offer now that makes my complicitness in this issue okay. But if you want to know why I spent ten years keeping these stories to myself, that's why. It was nothing more than survival. I kept my mouth shut so I could continue wearing the uniform. And I know I'm not the only one who picked the uniform over the cause.

There were days I listened to coworkers make disgusting comments about callers or victims. I ignored them when they talked about my breasts, my ass, and/or my legs. I laughed at sexual jokes and even made some of my own. I made my skin thick. I did my best to be one of the guys.

I made the mistake of wearing a skirt to a department event once and only once. It was a swearing-in ceremony for the new chief; if I remember correctly, we were told we had to attend. It was a hot day, and the ceremony was being held outside, in front of the building. I'd worked all night in the humidity, and my vest and uniform were damp with sweat. There was just enough time for me to go home and take a shower before having to be back for the ceremony.

The thought of putting my sweaty vest back on was enough to send me to my closet looking for dress-up clothes. Because of the warm weather, I thought a skirt might make me more comfortable. I picked out a knee-length pencil skirt and paired it with a three-quarter length sleeve shirt. I wanted to be comfortable, but I still wanted to look professional. It was the type of outfit you'd see a lawyer on TV wear.

I returned to the police department, overtired and overdressed. Immediately, I recognized my mistake. I had broken the code. I had put my femininity on display. My coworkers started making comments about my appearance. They feigned shock over my outfit and exclaimed how strange it was to see me "looking like a girl." They commented on how my legs and ass looked in my skirt and openly judged whether I was able to pull off the look. I'm sure it was all supposed to be funny, but it made me incredibly self-conscious.

They were judging me, after all. I saw them looking at me differently. I had temporarily broken the spell and reminded them I was not one of the guys but something different. I reminded them I was a woman.

It was a reminder that my position among them was not guaranteed. I realized I had to continue to prove, each and every day, that I belonged. I had to keep up appearances. I had to keep showing them how thick my skin was.

CHAPTER 6
FEMALE OFFICERS

Have you ever noticed you never use the term 'male officer' to describe a police officer?

Whenever I've mentioned this, someone is always quick to point out that since police work is a male-dominated profession, it's just assumed that a police officer is male.

Sure, maybe, that's true.

But statistically, 75% of teachers are women, but we don't say 'male teacher' when talking about them, so doesn't that kind of blow that argument?

I used this statistic in a conversation I once had, and the male I spoke with told me, "but it doesn't matter whether the teacher is male or female, so we don't need to define it."

I stared at him for a second, waiting for him to connect the dots for himself. When he didn't, I said "exactly."

He didn't understand.

It shouldn't matter whether a police officer is male or female. The job is the same. The job doesn't change based on gender. The only thing that seems to change is the level of respect.

There were more than fifty recruits in my police academy class, but only six of us identified as female.

The six of us were lodged in a different wing of the building, separated from the male recruits by stairs and halls. With all the stress put on uniformity, there was a big difference between the male and female recruits. Our academy experiences were completely different. Maybe not better or worse, but certainly different.

Most of the fourteen weeks I spent in the academy are now a blur of frog leaps and 'yes, sirs.' Of all the lessons and punishments and team-building exercises, the thing I remember most clearly was the way one of the cadre only referred to us as female officers or female cadets. Whenever he addressed the men in our class, he called them officers or cadets, but he always drew that line when he spoke to us.

That's what it felt like to me. A line was drawn in the sand, separating us into two sides.

Segregating us.

Dividing us.

He called us out, so we weren't part of the larger group but something different. Specifically, something less.

In the academy, they spend 75% of the time trying to scare the shit out of you. You want to believe that it's mostly about learning laws and important stuff like that, but it's not. The damned honest truth is that the whole thing is one big game, and they're just making sure you have what it takes to survive.

One of the techniques they used to scare us was showing us videos of worst-case scenarios. These were videos of the times when the bad guys won, and the good guys didn't go home. These were the reminders of the harsh reality of our chosen careers.

The videos were graphic. Officers got hurt. Officers died. Most were body camera footage or cruiser footage of savage attacks and ambushes. They were the kind of videos that still make me suck in my breath when I see one making its way around the Internet. The videos that break your heart, no matter how many times you've seen them, even when you know how it ends.

Some of these officers were killed by accident or killed doing absolutely nothing wrong. There were videos of officers doing everything they were trained to do and finding out it wasn't enough. But there were also videos of officers who made fatal mistakes.

We call them training videos.

As a police officer, I've watched hundreds of them over the years. We're expected to dissect them to see what the officers might have done differently to alter the results.

We're supposed to learn from their mistakes while hoping some other academy class isn't learning from our own mistakes someday in the future. We'd watch each video dozens of times in a row and then discuss the decisions, right and wrong, that ultimately led to the officer's name being added to the memorial wall in Washington, D.C. We played Monday morning quarterback with their final moments. It's a gut-wrenching way to learn.

In a way, though, I suppose the technique worked because I can still remember a lot of those officers. I remember how their voices sounded as they made their final, desperate radio calls. I remember forcing myself to keep my eyes open and watch for the small details that might someday save my own life. I remember the heavy quiet that would fill the room after a video ended the first time, an unspoken moment of silence for the fallen officer we never knew.

One specific video stands out in my mind from that day. Not because it was any more or less graphic than the others and not because the mistakes committed were any more egregious. I remember the video because the officer who died was a woman.

Despite being the only officer in the video, the cadre kept referring to her as 'the female officer' in the conversation that followed. He never referred to her by name or simply by the title officer. He always included the fact that she was female, as though somehow that biological fact was one of the mistakes that led to her death.

Her death was no more or less her fault than any of the other videos we watched. It was just as tragic, just as unnecessary. She was murdered, like hundreds of other officers in the line of duty. But even in death, it still seemed to matter that she was a woman.

The cadre harped on the word. "The female officer did this" or "what could the female officer have done when the bad guy did that?"

I kept waiting for him to say, "if she'd been a man, this never would have happened."

After that class, I approached this specific cadre. I openly shared my feelings about how he addressed the officer in the video and how he addressed the six of us who identified as women in the class.

I asked him to refer to us as officers, the same way he addressed all the other officers in our class. I asked him to stop drawing that line. I asked him to stop implying that we, as women, were any different than any other person wearing a uniform.

"No," he said flatly.

He left no room for further debate. He told me it didn't seem to bother anyone else, so I was perhaps too sensitive.

Sensitive.

The word stung. It's one of those words you never want to define you when you're a woman in a man's world. It correlates to weakness and inability. It's a career ruiner. Men don't take sensitive women seriously. Men don't want to work with sensitive women. Sensitive women don't have what it takes to be cops.

At that moment, I was reminded of the conversation I'd had with my training officer not long before. I needed a thick skin.

Apparently, even thicker than I had originally thought.

CHAPTER 7
"SHE'S ONE OF US"

I've been told more than once that I have a dirty mind.

Remember "that's what she said?" That was my kind of humor. I absolutely love when something completely innocuous sounds like a line from a spicy romance novel. It makes me laugh out loud. I can't help it.

I also happen to be a professional cuss word user. My mother doesn't always approve, but I use profanity in my daily life the way some people use salt on food. I sprinkle that shit on everything.

The combination of my admittedly immature humor and my proficiency in using the word 'fuck' quickly became something I was known for. Everyone knew they could make me laugh with a well-placed "that's what she said," and they knew I wouldn't be offended by foul language.

My dirty mind and an equally dirty mouth made my male coworkers more comfortable around me. On more than one occasion, when one of my coworkers introduced me to another officer from a different agency, they would follow the introduction with a little nudge and say, "don't worry, she's one of us."

Early on in my career, I prided myself on that distinction. I was successfully fitting in. I was "one of the guys." I was playing the game right, just like my FTO had taught me to do all those years before. That little nod felt like a gift of acceptance.

It took a long time, but I realize now that little nudge was really guy-code for, "she's not going to file a complaint with HR against you."

And they were right.

I never filed a single complaint during my career, but that doesn't mean I never had just cause. Looking back, there were many times when coworkers crossed the line with me, but I always allowed it. I had to allow it.

If I complained, I would have lost my hard-earned status of having thick skin. I never even considered filing a formal complaint with Human Resources against anyone, regardless of the behavior.

Somewhere along the way, "that's what she said" jokes opened the door to nastier, more uncomfortable forms of 'humor.' Simple sexual innuendos rapidly evolved into rape jokes. No one but me seemed to recognize the difference.

As a survivor of sexual assault, I don't find rape particularly funny. In fact, I find the idea that someone would laugh at sexual assault disgusting. But when everyone else was laughing, what was I supposed to do?

The stronger, more vocal, feminist version of myself I am today knows exactly what I should have done in those situations. But the young, naïve cop still focused on feeling accepted by her peers? She didn't have a clue. That version of me forced out the laugh. That version of me let everyone think I was 'cool with it.' That version of me wanted to stay 'one of them.'

Once I had committed to being one of the guys and letting that sort of humor go, there didn't seem to be any going back. On the one hand, I'd accomplished what I thought the goal was. I had established myself as the type of cop my fellow cops could be themselves around.

On the other hand, I lost a piece of myself. I sacrificed some of my own morals to be part of the group. The truth is, I permitted them to disrespect me. Every time they told one of those jokes or made one of those comments, they disrespected me, as well as women in general, and I never said a word. I just allowed it.

No one was afraid I would call them out on their bullshit because I never did. I was one of them and just as guilty as the rest. I was failing other women. I was failing myself. But I was one of the guys.

I recognize now that there's irony in having to sacrifice myself to let others be themselves. Especially if "being themselves" meant degrading and diminishing women.

That's the culture the male-dominated law enforcement world has cultivated.

It's a choice. Degrade yourself and fit in, or stand up for yourself and be outcasted.

I recognize now that I chose wrong, but I also don't blame the young version of me for making that choice. I don't blame any young officer who makes that decision. Given the alternative, the choice essentially makes itself.

CHAPTER 8
THE ONLY WOMAN IN THE ROOM

It wasn't unusual for me to look around a room and find that I was the only female present. It was pretty rare that I attended a training, briefing, or event where I wasn't the only woman in the room.

You have to have that tough skin when you walk into a room full of men, especially men you don't know. You know they're judging you. They're sizing you up and deciding right away whether or not you belong. They're likely not giving you the benefit of the doubt.

You can see it on their faces and hear it in their whispers. More than once, I've overheard other officers joking that I must have gotten lost en route to a different training. Surely I didn't belong in the tactics, firearms, or advanced drug recognition training.

I've heard the snickers and the coughs meant to cover laughs. There's even been a few guys who've dared to confront me directly, casually asking, "oh, are you here for XYZ class? Oh really? Wow. We figured you must have been confused."

I'd try to pretend I didn't see people double-take when they noticed me among the students. I tried not to get annoyed when people were genuinely shocked that I could hold my own in these classes. I bit my tongue when the instructor would offer backhanded compliments like, "Wow, you actually did really well today."

Unfortunately, this was just how it was most of the time.

Every time I showed up at a training, I had to be ready to prove myself all over again. I had to prove myself to my classmates, and I had to prove myself to the instructor.

Sometimes they let me win them over.

Sometimes they didn't.

I'm a life-long learner. I love being in the classroom and exploring new ideas. I love debating techniques and meanings. I love pushing myself to master new concepts. I loved attending training.

Some cops went to training as an "easy way" to get off the road for a day. They saw training as an opportunity to get paid to do very little work. They might not even care about the topic of the training. I once heard training referred to as a paid day off. Since trainings always took place between 0800 and 1700, it was also a way for an officer on the second or third shift to get an extra evening with their family.

All officers are required to do a certain number of training hours each year to maintain our certifications. Some officers just showed up to fulfill that requirement with no interest in what was being taught. For them, it was all about the certificate.

I didn't fall into either of these two categories. I liked training because it was training. I went to anything and everything I was offered. I took trainings on interview techniques and ground fighting. I took classes on drugs and mental illnesses. I took problem-solving and IED recognition. I took courses on domestic violence, sexual assault, and crimes against children. I took leadership classes and classes on search techniques. There wasn't a single topic I wasn't willing to learn about.

My favorite classes, however, were on tactics. I took every tactical class offered. I attended multiple different active shooter trainings. I took courses on tactical medical techniques and officer safety. Something about my brain loved working through the tactics of a scenario.

But tactics was an area even more coveted by men. It seemed to personally offend them that I would even consider stepping into this world.

At an active shooter training, an instructor assigned me to lead a team through a scenario. I was confident about the plan and knew I could successfully lead the team to complete our assigned mission. I quickly briefed my team in the same manner three of four team leaders had for different scenarios before me.

In those scenarios, the team leaders assigned jobs, answered relevant questions, and completed the exercise. Some of them had been successful. One of them had failed, and we had all learned from his mistake. Now it was my turn.

But my briefing was met with resistance. One of my team members declined his assignment and said he felt he would be of better use at a different post. A second team member argued with me about the strategy I had chosen. He thought I should implement his plan to be successful. The last team member said nothing, but he either didn't listen to me or hadn't agreed because he didn't do what I'd instructed him to do once we began.

The team failed the scenario. When my team members were asked why we had failed, they all blamed me.

"She didn't know what she was doing."

"She didn't give clear instructions."

"It was clear she's not a good leader."

I was mortified. Not only had my team failed, but they were now throwing me under the proverbial bus. I didn't stand a chance.

If you're waiting for the plucky turning point of this story where someone stands up for me and makes these guys look like jerks, you're going to be disappointed.

No one mentioned that the team failed because they refused to listen to me. No one mentioned that I was the only team leader whose team rebelled against the leadership. There was no sassy moment where everyone realized they shouldn't have underestimated me.

Instead, the instructor spoke down to me about needing to be a better leader because the survival of my team depended on it. We moved on to the next scenarios, where new team leaders took turns doing briefings without issues and gave me assignments that essentially equated to "try to stay out of the way."

Sometimes being the only woman in the room really sucked.

CHAPTER 9
LIKE A DAUGHTER TO ME

Early in my career, one of my sergeants took me under his wing. He frequently told me I reminded him of his daughters.

While this sounds endearing, it posed a very serious problem for me.

The sergeant's daughters were in grade school. When he looked at me, he saw a young, helpless girl who needed his protection, help, and guidance. He wasn't seeing me as a capable officer or an equal member of his squad. He consistently saw me as a child.

Since he was my direct supervisor, this created several issues.

On the one hand, my sergeant was kind and nurturing toward me. He wanted me to do my best and praised me when I did. He often expressed pride in my accomplishments and encouraged me to set high goals for myself.

We were also very close and had many deep conversations about work, the future, and life in general. He was like a father figure in many ways, mentoring me and guiding me toward what could be considered a successful future.

But on the flip side of that coin, my sergeant always treated me differently than the other officers on our shift. He would get frustrated or annoyed when I voiced independent opinions as if I was stubbornly talking back to him.

He got angry with me quickly and often scolded me the way you'd tell off a child for getting a bad grade. We once got in a heated screaming match over something likely inconsequential, and I remember how his face turned red as he yelled at me. Though it pains me to admit it, I cried as he screamed. From the outside looking in, we could have easily been arguing over a missed curfew or a dent in the bumper of the family car.

The truth of the matter is, while the relationship I had with this sergeant on a personal level was very special to me, professionally, it didn't work at all. He didn't respect me as an officer. He didn't see me in the same light as my coworkers. I was different. I was like a daughter to him, and that's not the ideal role for an officer to be placed in.

While this isn't the place to debate the patriarchal influences on the traditional family model, it's widely accepted that daughters and sons are often treated very differently. Daughters are 'treasured' for their beauty, kindness, and gentleness. It's the sons who are seen as the strong, capable workers. The daughters are seen as princesses, damsels in need of protection. The sons are the knights, training to be able to take care of princesses of their own someday.

It's awfully difficult to be taken seriously, especially in a world like law enforcement, when someone paints you as being like their daughter. And once one person has labeled you that way, the idea spreads.

Since I was only twenty-two when I started my career, most of my coworkers were significantly older than me. Most of them already had a decade or more of police work under their belts, and some were getting ready to retire. Based on age, some of them could have been my father.

The fact that this sergeant treated me like one of his daughters encouraged some of my other coworkers to view me in the same light.

Unfortunately, they weren't looking at me with the eyes of a proud parent. They saw me as too young, too incapable, too much of a princess.

The relationship with my sergeant gave some of the older men in my department an excuse to treat me with little or no respect. It was like my sergeant had brought me in for bring-your-daughter to workday, and the rest of them were humoring me by pretending I was a real police officer.

My "like-a–daughter" status only continued to reinforce that I wasn't their equal.

CHAPTER 10
SWAT

Five years into my career, spaces were available on the regional Special Operations Unit (SOU). In reality, it's a SWAT team, but New Hampshire prefers the gentler term of special operations.

While some departments in other parts of the country are big enough to house their own individual SWAT teams, towns in New Hampshire generally work together to create regional teams. The team consisted of officers from many participating agencies who trained together a few times a month. The team was activated to assist agencies in large-scale operations that the individual agency might not be equipped to handle alone, like barricaded subjects, search and rescue missions, or hostage situations.

There are two positions on the team: operators and negotiators. Operators are the boots on the ground, hands-on, busting down doors, people. The negotiators are hands-off, heard but not seen. They're both necessary and important parts of the team, but I wanted to be an operator. I wanted the action, up close and personal.

I announced my intentions to try out for the team, along with several other officers from my department. One of the officers was an older guy who'd recently retired from the NYPD. He came from the era of policing who believed women didn't belong on the street. He typically ignored my existence and rarely spoke to me, but when I announced my intention to try and make the team, he made a special exception.

"You can't be an operator," he snarled, literally disgusted with the thought. "Girls can't be operators. Put in for a negotiator. At least then you might have a chance."

I had no intention of changing my mind. I wanted to be an operator, and I would not be swayed. I was frustrated by the discouragement, but I chose to use it as fuel for my fire instead of letting it deter me. Call it my fatal flaw, but I was always willing to try and prove someone wrong.

After several interviews, I was selected for the team as an operator.

So was the officer who'd told me to try for the negotiators spot instead. I thought my appointment to the team would humble him, but it didn't. Instead, it seemed to make him angrier than ever.

Where before he simply didn't speak to me, now he refused to acknowledge me at all. He would go so far as to pretend I wasn't in the room and that he couldn't hear me when I spoke. He wouldn't drive to training with me, even though we were leaving from the same department. He pretended I didn't exist.

Not surprisingly, the team consisted entirely of men. Most of them were younger, in the realm of my age. They seemed accepting of me, though I suppose I'll never know what they were really thinking. At least they weren't outwardly disapproving.

To be on the team, you have to become SWAT Certified. This involves an intensive, two-week training. To send me to training, the team had to provide me with gear. Team members wear a heavier, more protective outer vest, a helmet and carry a variety of different equipment. The team's mission is different from that of the average patrol officer, so the tools are also different.

Unfortunately, the team didn't have equipment designed for my specific body type. The vest I was given was a 2XL. It might be hard to imagine how big that is, but picture this: I could sit on the ground and pull my arms and legs inside the vest like a turtle. I promise that's not how the vest should fit.

Because the vest was so large, it hung lower on my body than it should, reaching my midthigh instead of my waist. It covered my belt, meaning I couldn't use it to carry all the tools others might be able to carry there because I couldn't access it. I had to find other places to carry things. The vest also made it impossible to bend at the waist, which limited my mobility. And no matter how hard I tried, I couldn't cinch it tight enough to touch my body, so I was wider than I was used to being. This posed a problem when I went to walk through tight spaces, forgetting that I wasn't as narrow as usual.

Despite these difficulties, I excelled in SWAT school. I became the only active female SWAT operator in New Hampshire. It will always be one of my proudest accomplishments, mostly because it directly opposed what others believed I was capable of.

We were given pins to wear on our department uniforms, signifying we were members of this elite team. I wore mine proudly over my nameplate; two crossed arrows over a dagger.

The Lieutenant who had originally outfitted me with uniforms at the start of my career had since moved on to become the chief of a neighboring town. One day I happened to bump into him when he stopped into our department for something. He spotted the pin on my chest and was completely taken aback.

"You're on the SOU team?" he asked, shock and disbelief dripping from his words. When I confirmed that I was, he shook his head.

"Guess they're desperate for people these days, huh?" he said as he brushed by me.

It's painfully frustrating to be discounted even when you're succeeding. I know there was no truth to his words. Members of my department had been passed over for the spot on the team I filled. I know he said it only to cut me down. But knowing all that didn't change the way the words affected me in the moment. I can still hear them in my mind, full of venom.

It's taken me years to come to terms with the fact that you can't change sexist men just because you want to. There's no use in fighting with people like that Lieutenant or the coworker who ignored my existence. I would never change their minds about me, no matter how much I accomplished. To them, I would never be anything more than my gender.

And while I know that says more about who
they are than who I am, it can still be difficult
to swallow.

CHAPTER 11
THE FITNESS DOUBLE STANDARD

To be a police officer in the state of New Hampshire, there are specific physical fitness standards an individual needs to meet. New Hampshire's Police Standards and Training Council, the body that trains and oversees all of New Hampshire's law enforcement, chose to follow what is known as the Cooper Standards for determining physical fitness.

When I was hired, there were four requirements: a one-and-a-half-mile run, push-ups, sit-ups, and a bench press. At some point in my career, the council decided to drop the bench press from the standards, leaving the other three requirements as the requisites for becoming – and staying – a police officer.

The Cooper Standards determined how fast the run had to be finished, how much weight had to be bench pressed, and how many repetitions of the other exercises each person had to do to pass the physical fitness test. The standards are based on age and gender. The older someone is, the less that's required.

The Cooper Standards also hold those identifying as female to what many refer to as a lower standard than those identifying as male.

Females have longer to do the run and fewer required repetitions. Women are also allowed to perform modified push-ups, while men must do full-body push-ups. The justification for these differences is, of course, that the male body is designed differently than the female body. While males typically have stronger upper bodies, women tend to draw strength from their legs and hips.

I can't speak to the validity of the Cooper Standards research and have no knowledge of how they came into existence. I've been told they're the same standards the military used to design its PT standards, but I have no idea if that's actually true. All I know is these are the standards New Hampshire has in place for its police officers. These are the physical requirements I am asked to perform by the State.

If you ever want to see a man lose his mind, simply ask him about the "double-standard" of New Hampshire's physical fitness requirements.

I guarantee he'll rage about how women are given special treatment and complain about how all police officers have to do the same job, so all officers should have to hit the same requirements. He'll act personally offended by the difference in standards and talk passionately about how important the focus on equality needs to be.

Someone will comment every time the test is brought up. Sometimes the comments will be made under their breath. Other times they'll be framed as jokes. Sometimes they're just said with all the malice the person can muster.

Of all the times I've taken the PT test, I can't think of a single time when a man didn't mention the women's standards in a negative way. The comments were often directed at me as if I personally lobbied for the committee to pick these particular standards, even though they've been in place longer than I've been alive. Just being a woman, a "benefactor" of the lower standards, made me the enemy in their eyes.

For years I kept my mouth shut about the whole thing. After all, I didn't invent the standards. I am not Cooper, whoever Cooper happens to be. I didn't ask for lower standards or for someone to make a special exception for me. I was just born female, identify as female, and am therefore subject to the female standards.

For the record, both male and female candidates frequently fail their entrance PT tests. The standards are set to be at least somewhat challenging. I trained for months to be able to pass the entrance bench press, struggling to complete a single repetition of 75 lbs.

The Cooper Standards required you bench a certain percentage of your body weight. At the time I was applying, that equated to just under 75 lbs. But since weights don't typically come in half-pound increments, I was stuck rounding up to 75.

That may not sound like much, but I struggled with it. I failed at it the first time I applied at a department, having to leave with my tail between my legs as the other candidates headed out for the run.

I'd never been taught to bench press. No coach or gym teacher had ever brought me into a weight room. Even though I had been a student-athlete, I had always focused on running and ab exercises. Lifting weights was a whole new world for me.

Eventually, I was able to force up the single rep of 75 lbs, passing my department's candidate test and resulting in my hiring. Not long after, the bench press was dropped from the standards altogether.

After my initial introduction to weights, when I needed to learn to bench press, I became an avid weightlifter. I dabbled in body building, then spent a period as a competitive CrossFit athlete. I was strong, and I knew it. Every time I took a fitness test, I met and exceeded the standards for both a woman my age and a male my age.

It was important to me to be strong, not just because of the physical fitness test but because of the job.

Strong, in my mind, equated to capable. I believed that as long as I was physically strong enough to do any task I was asked to do, no one would be able to look at me differently. I worked hard to make sure no one would ever say, "she lost that fight because she's a girl."

Working out became an obsession for me. I spent six or seven days a week in the gym. I thought of it as part of my duty to myself and my fellow officers to be as strong as I could physically be.

I needed to be in shape.

I needed to be strong.

In my mind, the stronger I was, the less of a 'girl' I was. At some point, I started to believe the stronger I was, the more I would be respected.

But my strength never seemed to matter. Every time the PT test rolled around, there would be comments. It didn't matter that I chose to do full-body push-ups even though I could have done modified ones. It didn't matter that I did enough push-ups and sit-ups to meet the male standards. No one cared about what I actually did. They only cared about the fact that I could have done less.

I'm in absolute agreement that all police officers need to perform the same duties. As I've stressed, the job is the same regardless of who's doing it. Whenever I was asked, I always said I believed all officers should be held to the same standards.

But I would quickly follow that statement by arguing that I do not believe a long-distance run, push-ups, and sit-ups accurately represent the physical requirements needed to perform the job and should not be the standards used to determine our ability to be police officers.

For starters, in the ten years I worked the road as a patrol officer, I never once ran more than a few hundred feet in uniform. Foot pursuits, at least where I work, are not all that common. If there's a cop-out there jogging a mile and a half every day in uniform, they deserve a raise. But the reality is, most of the time, if an officer has to run, it's a short distance at a fast pace. A sprint as opposed to a marathon.

Sure, I understand there's an argument that the run is focused more on testing cardiovascular fitness than being directly duty-related. I agree that it's important for a police officer to have a healthy heart and lungs. I get it, I do. I just think there are better ways to test it.

While no one has ever asked for my opinion, this is my book, so I get to give it where I want to.

A duty-specific obstacle course is the best way to hold police officers accountable for their fitness. Create some events that relate to actual tasks an officer might have to perform on any given day. Have them climb over something, have them drag something, and have them pick something up and move it. Test their mobility, functional strength, and ability to go from a stand still to maximum effort with no warning. Many other states test their officers in duty-specific scenarios. There should be plenty of examples to choose from.

Once the state picks a test that is job function related, create a standard. Don't change it for age. Don't change it for gender. Say, "this is the standard to work as a police officer in our state, and if you can't meet it, you're not fit for the job." I think that's fair. After all, we all have to do the same job.

Do I think it's fair to say you have to be able to bench press 200 lbs to work here? No.

Even at the peak of my physical strength, I could never bench my bodyweight, which was the bare minimum standard for men. I know men who struggled with that standard. No matter how hard I pushed myself, I never developed my chest muscles enough to break my 115 lb. bench pressing plateau, and it took me years just to get to that point.

I'm glad the state finally did away with the bench pressing standard, not just because I struggled with it, but because it isn't job-related. I feel like removing that standard was a step in the right direction for the state to recognize that these tests are garbage, and hopefully, they will eventually scrap the whole damn Cooper thing. There have been rumors they're going to move away from it for years, but Cooper's still around every year.

The standards are lousy reflections of a cop's ability to perform the job, and I'm willing to bet a lot of great candidates have missed out on their opportunity to serve because of these stupid tests. But like I said before, no one has ever asked for my opinion on the matter, so what do I know?

A particularly vocal colleague of mine once brought up his disgust for the PT double standard as we were eating dinner. To be honest, I don't remember why the topic came up, but I do recall it being kind of out of the blue. He told me if I couldn't pass the test at the same standards as he did, I didn't deserve to be an officer.

I pointed out that I had passed all my PT tests at the same standard as he had, but he brushed that aside. Again, it wasn't about what I had done, it was about what I could have done. I could have done less, and that was the issue.

He went on to tell me that every officer in the state should be held to the standards of a twenty to twenty-nine-year-old male, without exception. His issue, like most others, was not with the tests themselves but with the standards. He wanted equality, mostly to ensure no one had it any easier than he did.

I asked him if he believed he'd still be consistently running a mile and a half in less than thirteen minutes when he was in his forties or older. He assured me that he would be.

I asked him if he had taken into account that he might, at some point, get injured or sick or have a surgery that might make it more difficult to meet that standard as a forty-year-old, hence why the standards flexed with age.

Again, I argued that because the tests weren't duty-related, it made sense to account for the fact that with age, it's not unusual for the body to slow down a bit, and that didn't necessarily mean someone wasn't fit to do their job. My colleague ignored my argument. He stated matter of factly that if someone couldn't pass the run in less than thirteen minutes, they should be fired on the spot.

(As a side note, I thought of this conversation recently when I was told that the same colleague had recently failed his run, despite being in an older age bracket and having more time to complete it. He used an injury as an excuse, but I couldn't help but wonder if he still felt anyone who couldn't finish the run in under thirteen minutes should be immediately fired.)

"They only flex the standards, so girls have a chance to pass. That way, agencies can hire a couple and say they have a diverse staff." He was practically spitting the words. "You're only here because you're a girl, and everyone cares about diversity now. You would never have been hired otherwise."

While this wasn't the most pleasant dinner conversation I'd ever had, it also wasn't the first time someone had played the diversity hire card when talking to me. In rural New Hampshire, there isn't a whole lot of diversity. Adding women to an agency's staff was often the only way to deviate from hiring white men with buzzcuts.

It had been thrown in my face more than once that being female was the only quality I had that justified my hiring. It wasn't my degrees, my judgment, my experience, or my personality. It was the fact that I had tits.

If men truly believed that women only got hired because they have breasts, why wouldn't the workforce be flooded with women? If nearly all women have breasts and most hiring authorities are men, wouldn't that mean they would hire all women to surround themselves with breasts?

Since that isn't the case and women are statistically not dominating the workplace, I have to reason that the boobs aren't as big of a factor as some people would like to believe. Which I guess is a good thing for me, since mine aren't very large.

But this is where the argument always ends up. We always circled back to the fact that the only purpose I was apparently serving my department was the addition of estrogen.

It's not easy to argue this point. I can't exactly argue that I'm not a deviation from the classically hired white male police officer.

I've also learned that no one making this argument wants to hear about my dual master's degrees or the experiences that made me a strong candidate. When someone truly believes the only purpose a woman serves is creating diversity, there's nothing that can be said to prove to them otherwise.

But knowing that doesn't make it any less frustrating when presented with the conversation. Since there's no winning this argument, you eventually have to swallow your pride and shut up.

Ultimately, you have to let the other person think they've won because there is literally no other way the conversation ends. They're never going to suddenly look up and say, "you know what, you're right! How have I been so stupid all this time?" You have to just let them win.

But damnit, I absolutely hate letting other people win.

CHAPTER 12
ACCORDING TO POLICY

The police chief that hired me had a stroke while I was in the police academy. He had been a police officer for more than 40 years and the chief of the department for longer than I'd been alive. Despite his tendency to be inappropriate, he'd had a long, respectable career. His stroke was devastating for the department.

An officer drove down to tell me and the other cadet from my department the sad news. He pulled us aside and told us the chief had survived but was in the hospital. No one knew what the future would bring to the department.

The chief underwent months of intensive physical therapy but could never fully regain his hands' use. He could not qualify with his firearm and, therefore unable to remain on the job. After he retired, an interim chief was named, and eventually, a nationwide job search was conducted to find a replacement. The process took forever. By the time the new chief was hired, I had been on the job for almost three years.

In the world of police work, three years is essentially around the time when an officer starts feeling comfortable. There's still a lot to learn, but there are no more 'rookie' mistakes. It's a good place to be.

I was happy.

I enjoyed going to work every day. The department wasn't perfect, but it felt like family. I felt like I was in the right place, and it seemed like my whole life had fallen into place. While I had originally been incredibly homesick after making the two-hour move north from my hometown, I now felt I had a new home.

I planned to do my entire career in the town, like many of the officers who outranked me. It isn't common practice for officers to spend their whole careers in one place, so the fact that so many had chosen to do so in our department spoke to the quality of the workplace. I was looking forward to a long career.

The new chief came with promises of exciting changes. He had big plans to make the department an even better place. He discussed implementing some much-needed forward progress into our somewhat outdated ways. He talked about making the department stronger than it had ever been. He said all the right things and told us exactly what we wanted to hear. Everyone was excited.

Unfortunately, we learned pretty quickly the new chief was more of a politician than a leader. The progressive changes he promised were buried under new paint and motivational posters. He focused on superficial issues and ignored our deeper concerns. He created committees to have discussions that never amounted to anything and talked about things that created nothing more than false hope. Morale dropped, and the close-knit family feel the department had once had slipped away.

One change the chief did manage to implement was creating new policies. The chief was pursuing accreditation, a shiny stamp of approval that would claim our department was doing everything right. Accreditation required specific new policies and the rewriting of old ones. Admittedly, some of the department's policies needed updating. While accreditation wasn't the first thing we had hoped the new chief would tackle, the updating of policies seemed like a positive step in a forward direction.

Each week, the chief would put out a handful of new policies we would have to read and sign, acknowledging that we understood and agreed to follow them. It became apparent quickly that many policies were just copied and pasted from other departments around the state. Some of them were the same as our original policies, just using fancier words and better letterhead.

Most people didn't even bother to read them; they just skimmed the page and signed at the bottom. But I'm a nerd, so I read each new policy. As I read through them, I noticed many of them contained phrasing that held male and female officers to different standards. Some of them went so far as to enforce requirements, like stating a female officer would be present at all recruiting events. The wording in many of the policies seemed to reinforce the gender divide between the male and female officers. The more I read, the more alarm bells went off in my head. I wasn't comfortable signing off on policies I disagreed with.

The new chief had stressed that his door was always open, so I took the policies to him with the notes I had made on my concerns. I pointed out the implications and suggested changes that would eliminate the issues. My degrees are in writing, so I felt pretty comfortable discussing the documents. I was in my element.

The chief stared at me across his desk like I had just walked in and slapped him across the face with a fish.

He told me that he didn't understand my concerns, saw no issue with the wording, and assured me that the policies were in line with the "best practices" of police work. He then dismissed me and asked me to close his door on the way out.

I was surprised at his reaction, but I was not deterred. I can be a bit stubborn when I want to be, and this was a hill I had chosen to die on.

I did not sign off on any of the policies I had concerns about. Instead, I began calling around to various other agencies in the state, asking for copies of similar policies and comparing the wording.

In only a few days, I had compiled a collection of policies for agencies similar to ours, as well as some of the biggest agencies in the state. Despite the chief's initial claim that his new policies followed best practices, I couldn't find a single other agency that used similar language or created similar requirements.

I assumed when I met with the chief this time, armed with my research, he would have to see my point. Unfortunately, my plan backfired. He was furious that I had gone behind his back and contacted other agencies regarding the policies. He flat out refused even to hear my argument or look at the documentation I had collected. He then ordered my sergeant to have me sign off on the policies in question or be found insubordinate.

Defeated, I signed off on the sexist policies.

As I got to know the chief, I noted that he often displayed sexist behaviors. There was nothing egregious; he was too polished of a politician for that. The behaviors he'd developed were subtle.

There was nothing I could point to and say, "See, I told you!" but plenty of instances that left me feeling minimized. It was one of those things that was impossible to put into words but also couldn't be denied. That feeling you can't explain but also can't ignore.

I knew the chief was sexist, but I also knew I'd never be able to prove it.

CHAPTER 13
THE LAST STRAW

The chief announced he was going to promote a new sergeant. There was going to be a selection process, which involved a written test and an assessment center. An assessment center is essentially a collection of mock scenarios used to grade a person's capabilities at handling certain situations.

I met all the basic requirements for the position. I was nervous about applying, but other officers encouraged me. Since we were short-staffed, I was already running the shift that was missing a sergeant. According to a few of my trusted colleagues, the decision to promote me was a no-brainer.

The first step was to submit a letter of intent. I carefully crafted my letter, highlighting the role I was already filling and the qualifications I had developed during my time on the job. I submitted my letter and began preparing for the written exam.

There were several dense and outdated textbooks the chief had chosen to focus the exam on. I studied the textbooks for weeks leading up to the test, and even though I felt many of the texts did not directly relate to the style of policing our department required, I passed the test.

I soon learned I was the only officer to pass the written test. Failing the written test disqualified anyone else from moving forward to the assessment center.

One of the officers who failed had several more years on the job than me. He was not the type of man who viewed women in law enforcement as his equal, and it was clear he was unhappy that I had done better than he had. Clearly, he had believed he was the obvious choice for the promotion. There were even rumors that it had been promised to him. But, promises or no promises, he hadn't fulfilled the chief's requirements. He was no longer eligible for the promotion.

I moved on to the assessment center alone. The assessment center was run by an outside agency that had been hired to conduct a fair, unbiased assessment. The problem was that the assessment was run by two men who had made their decision about me before I even started the scenarios. They spoke down to me, belittled me, and ultimately rated my performance extremely poorly.

They used all the buzzwords for female leaders when telling me how poorly I'd done. They described me as too aggressive and bossy in one scenario and then too passive and inept in another. They questioned basic decisions I made and dismissed my justifications. They said I lacked leadership qualities, despite statements to the contrary from those I actually interacted with daily.

While their review disheartened me, I figured the chief would put more stock into what I had already demonstrated to him through my daily work within the department. After all, these outsiders weren't actually the ones making the promotion decision. I knew I had the skills and abilities to be a sergeant in the department.

This was not a quick process, even though I was the only person involved. The entire thing took months. When the chief finally summoned me to his office, I was full of nervous energy. I donned a fresh uniform and polished the silver of my badge and belt buckle for the meeting. I arrived forty minutes early and paced the squad room until it was finally time to hear the chief's decision.

The new chief occupied the same corner office where I signed my initial offer to become a police officer. While the previous chief had met with me at a small round table in the corner, this chief sat across from me, his large desk dividing us. The newly hired captain sat to the Chief's left, perched awkwardly on the edge of a chair. Neither one of them looked pleased to be meeting with me. It wasn't a very welcoming environment.

First, the chief pulled out the letter of intent I had written months earlier, stating my intentions to join the promotional process. He pointed to a section he had highlighted, where I stated that I had been working for the department for five years.

"Why did you lie here? You have not been working for the department for five years."

I was completely taken off guard by the question. This was not at all what I was expecting. I tried to wrap my head around what he was asking - or accusing - me of.

I was hired in September of 2012. It was the summer of 2017. I don't remember the exact date, but it was not yet September. Technically, I had not yet reached my five-year anniversary. I hadn't intended to lie. I had quite literally taken 2017, subtracted 2012, and got the number five. I hadn't put any thought into the months and exact date.

I explained this and apologized for any confusion. Since the promotion requirement was only three years on the job, it didn't seem like the stretch of a few months placed me in any danger of not being qualified.

The chief put the letter down on his desk and folded his hands on top of it. He told me he would not be offering me the promotion. He told me he didn't think I was qualified for leadership and that he did not see my career with the department advancing beyond where I currently was. He then handed me a generic memo telling me I had not been promoted and offered no further explanation.

I was devastated.

Yes, I was hurt that I hadn't been chosen for promotion, but it was more than that. It was the fact that the chief had diminished everything I had done up until this point in my career. He invalidated me, and I knew exactly why.

I'll never be able to prove it, but I know I wasn't offered that promotion because I'm a woman. It never had anything to do with my skills or abilities. At the end of the day, the chief never intended to promote me.

The chief reposted the position a week after turning me down for promotion. This time, he changed the evaluation process and removed the written test. The officer that had previously failed the written test was suddenly the perfect candidate for the job. He was promoted a short time later.

People dismissed me whenever I tried to point out the strange circumstances surrounding the promotional process. They said I was just bitter because I hadn't been promoted.

No one wanted to hear that the process seemed sexist at worst and rigged at best. I had been disappointed not to be promoted, but I wasn't bitter. I just wanted to be heard.

I wanted someone to acknowledge that it wasn't right to change the standards so you could hire the person you intended to hire all along. I wanted someone to recognize that the chief had never given me a valid reason not to promote me. I just wanted someone to listen.

Although I knew I had nothing concrete to report, I finally went to the town administration with my concerns regarding the chief. In a closed-door meeting with an administrator I trusted, I said, "the chief of police is sexist."

The administrator looked me square in the eyes and said, "I know, but we're working on it."

I was dumbfounded.

Here was a woman who had clawed her way to the top of a patriarchy, acknowledging that the man she put in charge of the police force was sexist, but all she could do was offer me a placating shrug and promise they were working on it.

How does one work on being sexist? Do you take vitamins for that?

That was when I knew my career in the town I loved was over.

I began looking at other departments for openings, which felt like a betrayal to the other officers I worked with. Even though the new chief had killed the family atmosphere within the walls, I still felt loyalty to the brothers I had there.

Looking at other departments felt like the death of a dream. I had intended to work my whole career on the streets of the town that hired me. I had started there, I had grown there, I had wanted to stay there.

But leaving was the only option I felt I had.

The atmosphere had become so toxic that I could feel it negatively affecting my mental health. While I had faced a lot of sexism and sexual harassment up to that point, I couldn't bare to work under such hostile leadership.

I had lost all respect for the man sitting in the corner office. I was even beginning to lose the ability to fake respect for him. I knew I needed to leave.

CHAPTER 14
TRAINING

As I mentioned earlier, I had become very used to being the only female in the room when I attended trainings. Because you're required to attend so many hours of training each year, there are generally a lot of training options to choose from. Some of these trainings are hosted by the academy, but there is a wide range of classes that can count toward training hours.

There are the officers looking for easy trainings, hoping to coast through the hours and check off their training box for the year as quickly as possible with as little effort as possible. They usually pursued trainings hosted by the academy. Eight hours of sitting in the classroom and watching PowerPoint slides, ending in a handshake and a certificate.

I usually looked for more hands-on trainings than the basic academy classes. I actively pursued trainings in areas that interested me and areas I felt I could improve in. I was always looking to make myself a more valuable member of the department and an overall better officer.

So when I saw the advertisement for a two-day course called "Woman in Command" I was ecstatic. The course was specifically geared toward women in the male-dominated field of law enforcement. The course was designed like a small conference, and it promised to address topics that were of direct concern to female officers.

I'd never heard of anything like it in my years on the job. As I'd just been passed over for promotion because I supposedly lacked leadership skills, this seemed like the perfect course for me.

In order to attend trainings, an officer has to get approval from the command staff. A lot of trainings are free to attend, so the person in charge of approving trainings, which was the Captain in my department at the time, would just need to verify that the course didn't interfere with road coverage before approving attendance. Some courses included admission fees or travel costs, but departments generally budget for these types of costs.

I was lucky to work for a department with a large training budget. Officers were rarely denied training opportunities, regardless of cost. It wasn't uncommon for officers to travel around New England for various trainings. We'd even sent officers as far as Arizona.

The Women in Command course did have an admission fee, but it was reasonable. It was being held approximately two hours away in Massachusetts, so it was hardly a long haul. The course brochure was packed with valuable content. I was confident when I submitted my request to attend, it would be approved.

A week later, however, I received the denial.

The submission form was returned to my mailbox with only the words "doesn't appear applicable" scratched on it. For my life, I couldn't figure out what part of the class didn't apply to my job. It was a conference designed for women who worked in law enforcement and wanted to be leaders. It couldn't have been more applicable to me if it had my name in the title.

I attempted to speak to the captain about the denial, but he refused to discuss it further. All he would say was that the department would not send me to a training that didn't seem relevant to my work.

Though the department seemed to feel the training wasn't relevant, I couldn't have disagreed more. At the encouragement of one of my sergeants, I decided to attend the training on my own time. I took the two days off as vacation, paid for my registration, and traveled on my own dime.

On the first training day, I walked into the banquet hall and looked around. I was surrounded by almost two hundred other women police officers from all over New England and as far away as Canada.

The feeling was surreal.

In my entire career, I had never seen so many women officers in one place. I had spent six years always being the minority in the room, but standing in that banquet hall was the first time I didn't feel alone.

The conference was an amazing experience, and if you're a woman in a male-dominated line of work and you ever get the opportunity to attend something like this, take my advice and GO!

I could openly discuss the experiences I'd been having and have my feelings validated. I learned from other women who had dealt with similar issues. I was able to speak freely and be myself. It was the first and only time in my career that I felt completely understood in a room full of police officers.

When the conference ended, I returned to my department feeling more confident about my decision to move on. Through conversations with the other attendees, I recognized that it wouldn't matter what I did to improve myself, I would never be able to overcome my gender in the eyes of that particular police chief.

I felt heard.

I felt validated.

I felt empowered.

We talked about things we'd never mention in front of our male coworkers, like how sexual harassment and sexism made us feel.

Because of this conference, I feel confident that I'm not alone in feeling like an HR complaint would be career suicide. It was a universal feeling in the room. It was something we all just got.

But for those two days, I didn't have to pretend to be one of the guys. I didn't have to worry about having thick skin or hiding my femininity. For those two days, I could be myself and be a police officer. It was amazing.

Truthfully, it was probably the most important training I took throughout my entire career. It was certainly a lot more relevant to my work than the final training that the chief would ever send me to before I left his command.

Since you're reading my book, you may have noticed I'm a writer. Usually, I don't like to brag about my achievements, but to fully grasp the ridiculousness of this next story, you have to understand my background fully.

Most people assume you have to have a degree in criminal justice to become a police officer, but that's actually not true. My degrees are in English and writing. Yes, I said degrees, plural. I completed my bachelor's degree in English with a concentration in writing and went on to get a master's degree in English and Writing. I also have a Master of Fine Arts in Creative Writing and a graduate certificate in teaching writing. Add in the fact that I was also an editor for my college newspaper and a writing tutor, and you might be able to say I've got a little experience in writing.

This was not a secret in my police department. My nerdiness was a running joke, but when officers struggled with reports or warrants, they would bring them to me for review. This was not part of my official job, of course, since I hadn't been promoted, but even the sergeants asked me to look over their work from time to time.

The prosecutor told me multiple times how much he loved my police reports because they were so well-written and detailed. He once told me several defense attorneys had declined to take my cases to trial because my reports were so well written. I would argue that I knew what I was doing in the report writing area.

Since the department had refused to send me to the Women in Command training, they seemed to be under the impression they needed to send me to something else.

The chief decided to send me to a three-day basic report writing course. It was literally titled Report Writing: 101.

I am not about to sit here and tell you I know everything there is to know about the written word. I make mistakes. Maybe you've even found one in this book. There is always more to learn when it comes to language and writing, and I am always happy to improve my skills. However, this was not an opportunity for me to learn new things.

This course was so introductory, it started with the basic sentence and paragraph structure. Most of the students in the class were within their first year on the job and learning to write reports for the first time. For some, they seemed to be learning to write in general for the first time.

I was six years into my career and had more writing experience than the instructor.

When I asked the chief why he was sending me to basic report writing, he gave some vague response about how it was a good opportunity. He would not discuss it further with me.
The class was held in my department, and I was the only officer required to attend, despite there being several officers who actually might have benefited from a back-to-basics writing refresher.

I tried to clarify with the chief how attending a female-empowered leadership class was not relevant to me, but wasting my time in a class about writing in complete sentences was. Still, he wasn't interested in offering a justification.

CHAPTER 15

DARLING, SWEETIE, BABY, HONEY

You've probably seen dozens and dozens of police officers in your lifetime. Maybe you've just seen them in passing, perhaps you've had small interactions with them, maybe you've been arrested by one or two. Regardless of who you are, I'd be willing to bet your path has crossed with a handful of men or women in uniform at some point.

As a police officer, I interacted with members of the public multiple times a day, all day long. Interactions could last anywhere from a few seconds to hours at a time. Interacting with the public is probably the biggest part of the job.

Not every interaction I had with someone from the public was bad. In fact, I would say more than 80% of my daily interactions were positive.

I might run into a store to grab a drink and chat with the other patrons. I might stop at the library and meet a few kids. Sometimes while I was sitting in my parked cruiser, people would walk up to introduce themselves or ask questions. Having conversations with all sorts of different people was one of the things I enjoyed about my job.

What I didn't enjoy about interacting with the public, however, was how often someone would call me sweetie, baby, darling, sweetheart, sugar, baby girl, doll, or some other disgusting term of endearment. Anything you can think of, I've been called.

Have you ever looked at a man wearing a uniform and thought about calling him 'honey'? I mean, a completely random man you've never met who is carrying a gun and wearing a bulletproof vest. Does that seem like the person you walk up to and say, "good morning, babe, can you give me directions to South Street?"

I'm willing to bet that you have never had that urge. In fact, you probably approached that man and said, "excuse me, sir?" or perhaps you went with the always safe, "hello officer, could you help me?"

Your first instinct is probably to show that man some respect. He's a police officer, after all.

Despite the fact that I was wearing the exact same uniform, carrying the same gun, and sitting in the same car, folks never seemed to think they needed to show the same level of respect when addressing me.

Yes, before some of you get all huffy, I will concede that there are some people who use these terms as part of their normal language. While I think there is room to debate whether that's appropriate, we can factor in that a small percentage of people might actually call everyone by these pet names. A small percentage.

I will argue that it isn't the norm for people in Northern New Hampshire. We're just not that type of place. The waitresses at our local restaurants don't call everyone sweetie. The cashiers don't call everyone honey. We're a small town, but we're not that small town.

But even factoring in the odd person who might have an excuse, an astounding number of people addressed me using terms like baby, sweetie, doll, and sugar each and every day.

There's a specific type of person who likes to use these types of terms to talk to women in positions of authority. It's the same type of person that acts surprised to see a woman in a police uniform and says things like, "oh, I had no idea this town had female officers. How nice!"

I was never quite sure how people expected me to respond to that.

Do you want my autograph?

Does being a woman and a police officer make me some kind of spectacle?

Perhaps the town should have been paying me more since I was also doubling as a tourist attraction.

These were the same types of people who would call the police department and ask to speak to the officer on duty. When I would tell them I was the officer on duty, hence why I introduced myself as Officer Corcoran, they would say, "wait, really?"

It sometimes felt like people went out of their way to work these terms into the conversation. Once while directing traffic at an accident scene, a man slowed down, rolled down his window, and said, "thanks, sweetheart," before driving away.

On another occasion, a woman had to wait for a traffic light to change, cross the street, and wade through a crowd of people to say, "Hello dear, don't you look nice in your uniform?" like I was a Girl Scout selling cookies and not an armed police officer walking down the street of the town I was sworn to protect.

And these, of course, are examples of the people you can argue were being nice!

I would guestimate that more often than not, when I approached a situation in an official capacity, someone would address me by one of these terms in an attempt to 'put me in my place.' While this was most often a tactic used by men, it wasn't uncommon to have a woman deploy it either.

"Well, you see, sweetheart..."

"Okay, hun."

"Sorry to waste your time, doll."
(Doll? Who even says that anymore? What is this, the fifties?)

And of course, this is another example of a no-win situation.

If I responded with something like, "I'm not your baby, don't call me that," the individual would usually puff out their chest and say something like, "I'm just trying to be nice, I didn't mean anything by it, you women are all so sensitive, blah blah blah."

Now that I've alerted the asshole that the use of the pet name bothers me, and he thinks he has the power. He's obviously not going to stop using the term. If anything, he'll start using more.

Can't win in that direction.

But by choosing to ignore the fact that he's saying it, he thinks you like it. He gets that weird ego masculinity that makes him feel important and tough. That also encourages him to continue with vigor.

Can't win that way either.

It's obnoxious.

Then there are the men who are using the terms like threats. They're usually angry, probably did something wrong, and they think they're badasses that can get away with whatever they want.

They say things like, "Listen, babe, I know you think you know what's going on here, but...." They spit the term out, and there's no mistaking the intentions of the terminology.

It's a reminder. They're trying to make a point that they're the man and I'm the woman. They're making it perfectly clear that they have zero respect for me.

These are usually the same guys who ask when "the real police" will show up. They try to speak over me, and if I have a male partner on the scene, they'll try to only speak to him instead of me.

These are definitely not terms of endearment when these types of people are wielding them. For these guys, they're insults. They might as well be calling me a slut or a whore, the way they throw them out is the same.

For these types of people, it's all about control and power. I'm supposed to have the power because I'm the one in uniform, but because I also happen to be a woman, they can't allow that.

Sorry to be the barer of bad news, but there's no winning with these types of men either. Speak to them too kindly, and they assume you're a pushover. Try to show authority, and they whine that you're being a bitch to them.

Lose-lose.

Much of my job was balancing how to talk to all these different types of people. I had to develop strategies and different techniques for every kind of person. It's not like I could throw my hands up and walk away when I was frustrated. I didn't get to pick and choose which types of people I dealt with. If I was dispatched to the call, I had to resolve it, whether the people I was dealing with were assholes or not.

My male colleagues never understood this. For them, dealing with men who disliked authority ultimately was a pissing match. They'd all puff out their chest until either the bad guy backed down or he crossed the line that would get him arrested. End of story.

I never had that luxury. I couldn't just have a male coworker show up whenever a guy was sexist. Police work just doesn't work that way. No one could teach me how to deal with these scenarios because no one else was experiencing them. I had to figure it out on my own.

The most annoying thing about it was it took so much patience.

I'm willing to bet that sometimes calls like this took me two or three times longer than they would have taken my coworkers because I had to talk the person in circles until they were doing what I wanted them to do, but they believed it was their idea. Showing up with authority just wasn't always enough.

I once mentioned my various police personalities to a coworker who couldn't wrap his mind around it. He had just had to be a tough cop for his entire career. He didn't know how to be calm cop and gentle cop and nice cop and bitch cop and patient cop and play-dumb cop and all the other versions of cop I had to use on a daily basis just to do the job.

"That sounds exhausting," he'd said.

All I could say in response is, "you have no idea."

CHAPTER 16

"WHAT ARE YOU, HIS SECRETARY?"

While the pet names can be obnoxious, they're slightly better than the lectures. These usually came from men I'd arrested, but occasionally they came with no prompting at all.

More than once, I arrived at a call and had a man refuse to speak with me. Once, a man called 9·1·1 to report a theft. When I arrived to take the theft report, he refused to speak to me about his situation. He demanded a different officer be dispatched to take his report. He wanted someone "knowledgeable."

Unfortunately for this gentleman, that's not how filing a police report works.

You get who you get; in this case, he got me. I explained to him that I was the officer here to take his report, and if he didn't want to give his report to me, he would not be able to make a report that night.

He wanted to speak to the shift supervisor, which I got the pleasure of telling him was also me.

He was furious. After shutting the door in my face, he called dispatch back and demanded a different officer. Dispatch told him there were no other officers available, only me. He still refused to speak to me, so he did not file his report that evening.

It sounds so stupid. You're probably thinking to yourself, "that can't possibly have really happened. What kind of a person is that stupid?" But these are the kinds of things I regularly dealt with. These are the types of things that happened to me weekly, sometimes daily. The types of things my male coworkers have never even imagined having to deal with.

None of my coworkers had ever been turned away at the door because of their gender. No one ever called for an officer and then refused to speak with them when they showed up. When I tell them stories like this, they're baffled. They can't wrap their minds around it.

Some of them have seen it firsthand, so they have an idea of what I deal with, but they still don't fully get it.

I once had to arrest a drunk veteran, probably for disorderly conduct or some other minor offense. It was an inconsequential arrest. I shouldn't remember anything about this man or his arrest, except he was such a flaming asshole, he burned himself into my memory.

As I was arresting him, he kept yelling that he was a veteran and that I didn't have any right to arrest him. Being a veteran does not exempt you from being arrested, but I have heard it yelled a time or two before. That's not the behavior that cemented this guy into my memory.

In the booking room, he launched into a lecture about how he knew women just like me in the military, and we're all the same. According to him, women in the military and women in law enforcement were power-hungry bitches. We abuse our authority to feel important, but everyone knows we're useless sluts.

It was a frustrating narrative, to say the least, but I tried to push through. I started the booking process, which is entirely administrative. It consists of filling out the booking paperwork, taking a booking photo, and doing fingerprints. In a good situation, it's pretty quick. With a cooperative arrestee, you can get them in and out in half an hour.

This gentleman was not the definition of cooperative.

He refused to answer or acknowledge any of the questions I asked him, which were demographic: name, date of birth, height, and weight. We're not talking about deep conversations here.

Instead of responding, he raved about my inferiority and power complex, talking right over my attempts to complete the incredibly simple process.

Finally, out of frustration, I had another officer join me in the booking room. Suddenly, this man's entire demeanor changed. He sat up straight and stopped ranting. He sat quietly and answered each question the other officer asked, saying 'yes, sir' or 'no, sir.'

I quietly stewed as I typed in the answers to each question I had already asked a dozen times. When my coworker stepped out of the room, the man said, "I knew it. You're just his secretary. So typical, trying to act more important than you are. Fucking bitches."

I had to leave the room.

I was so appalled at this man's behavior. I have the utmost respect for our country's veterans. I always have and always will. My father and brother served in the military, so I'm not unfamiliar with the challenges veterans face and the sacrifices they make. But I could not generate respect for this man.

I can still picture him ranting and raving about how useless women in service were and how the world would be better off without us in the military and law enforcement.

However, my coworker's reaction to him was almost as bad as the man himself. He laughed about it later, finding humor in the fact that the man would only respond to him.

"Sexist prick," I said later, as my coworker retold the story to the oncoming shift hours later.

"It's not sexist," he said with a laugh, "that dude's just a drunk asshole."

I think my mouth literally fell open. Was he not in the same room as me? Was he thinking of a different drunk? Why give that misogynist dick the benefit of being a drunk asshole? Excusing his behavior as anything else is just justifying it further.

But no one seemed to see it that way. They were just the antics of a drunk who was pushing my buttons.

"Don't be so sensitive," my coworker said. I cringed at the word. I knew I wasn't being "too sensitive." The man had gone on for hours about women and me specifically. He'd checked every box in the sexist book. Why couldn't they give me the benefit of agreeing?

Why, even when it was an arrestee, did my coworkers have to make excuses for the behavior?

CHAPTER 17
WOMEN LIKE YOU ARE THE PROBLEM

I preface this story by saying, traffic enforcement wasn't my thing. Every cop has a thing that they just really enjoy doing. Some officer's really love traffic enforcement. They like stopping cars for various violations. That's their thing.

I was never one of those cops. The only reason I ever stopped cars was because my boss told me I had to. Minor traffic violations were just not that big of a deal to me. When I did stop cars, it was with the hope that I might be able to dig deeper than just the traffic violation. I would rather stop someone from driving drunk than lecture them about having a headlight out.

Since it wasn't my thing, I didn't write a lot of tickets. I was, and still am, of the opinion that a warning is often just as effective as a ticket. So ninety-nine times out of a hundred, much to my chief's dismay, I let people off with warnings.

One night, I was running radar in a 35 MPH zone. It was late and there wasn't a lot of traffic. A car came by doing 49 and I figured that was good a stop as any for that hour. Before I even got out of my cruiser, I had every intention of giving the driver a warning. I frequently gave warnings to people going a lot faster in the same exact place, so I had no plans to jack this driver up for 14 MPH over the limit.

The driver was a woman about the same age as I was. She had been talking to her boyfriend using the Bluetooth in her car at the time of the stop, which I didn't know but shouldn't have mattered. Using Bluetooth while driving was perfectly legal in New Hampshire as long as the driver isn't physically holding or manipulating the phone.

When I approached the driver's window, I identified myself and let her know why I had stopped her. I never played that "do you know how fast you were going" game. I simply told her she was doing 49 in a 35 and asked for her license and registration.

Instead of getting her information out for me, she started complaining to her boyfriend that I was stopping her for doing 49 in a 40 MPH zone. Her Bluetooth was coming through her car's stereo system, so I could hear him loudly saying that was bullshit.

I made the mistake of trying to correct her. I explained that the area where I stopped her, which was directly in front of a school, was actually a 35 MPH zone, not a 40. She argued with me, playing the "I grew up here, and I know everything about this town" card. She told me the road was a 40 MPH road and that she should know because she'd been driving that road her whole life.

I figured instead of continuing with the pointless argument that this woman clearly wasn't going to relent on, I'd point out that even if the area was a 40 MPH zone, she was still doing 49, which was still speeding, and I still needed her license and registration.

At that point, the woman's boyfriend came across the speakers, yelling about how I stopped his girlfriend for driving "only" nine miles per hour over the speed limit. He started an angry rant, yelling about how I was abusing my power as a police officer and how this was obviously a speed trap.

I tried to ignore the boyfriend, seeing as he wasn't even in the car. I asked the woman for her identification again.

The boyfriend, apparently not liking the fact that I wasn't engaging with him via Bluetooth, exploded. He yelled, "women like you are the problem with this world. You're out there trying to prove you're tough because you know you don't belong in a field like police work. Why don't you go be a nurse or something where you belong?"

I was astonished when instead of trying to quiet her boyfriend, the driver turned up the volume on her car's stereo. He continued berating me via the sound system while I tried to get the driver's information. Even after she gave it to me, finally allowing me to walk back to my cruiser, he didn't stop his rant.

According to this woman's boyfriend, women were constantly trying to force their way into power when they obviously didn't belong there. Law enforcement, the military, politics. Women like me were the problem.

The driver had no history, and despite the behavior, I still had every intention of giving her a warning. It was a minor violation, one I'm sure I've been guilty of many times myself. I returned to the car window to return the driver's license and registration. As soon as I told the driver I was giving her a warning for the speed, the rant erupted again.

Obviously, I had realized my mistake, and I was trying to save face now, he said. His girlfriend should sue, they could get me fired.

The woman snatched her license and registration away from me and pulled away before I'd even finished talking. I could still hear her boyfriend yelling as she drove off. While I had managed to remain professional throughout the entire encounter, on the inside, I was fuming.

I was mad about the things the boyfriend had said, but the truth is, it's nothing I hadn't heard a hundred times. It always annoyed me, but it was hardly unusual. It was the first time I'd ever gotten the speech via Bluetooth, but that's not what pissed me off either.

What truly infuriated me was that this woman just let it happen. Her boyfriend was being overtly sexist, and she didn't even care. On the contrary, she turned up the volume to ensure I could clearly hear every word. I couldn't imagine how she could endorse him, saying that women in men's jobs were the problem with society. It enraged me.

For some reason, her reaction was what makes that stop stand out in my mind all these years later. How could she not be ashamed or offended?

CHAPTER 18
RUMORS

There's a severe shortage of women among the ranks of the nearby police departments, but there was no shortage of gossip about the few there were. I could count on one hand how many other women patrolled the nearby streets.

Despite being outnumbered ten to one, there seemed to be nothing else worth talking about besides what they were doing with their personal lives.

Someone was sleeping her way through the department. Someone was having an affair with a commanding officer. Someone was sleeping with too many men, and someone else wasn't sleeping with enough.

For a profession that relies so heavily on facts to do the job, everyone was always quick to spread rumors with zero regard for whether there was any evidence to support what was being said.

I quickly learned that no matter what you're doing, someone's going to think you're doing the wrong thing.

As I adapted to life as a police officer, I tried to keep my head down. I heard plenty of stories about women who'd come before me and destroyed their futures before they were even off probation. I was determined to keep my head down and avoid becoming a cautionary tale.

But despite my attempts to blend in, rumors quickly seemed to develop about me. No one ever seemed to know where they originated from, but everyone seemed to have heard them. And while everyone swore they hadn't passed the rumors on, they somehow still managed to swirl around the department. I was still on FTO when the first rumor hit me.

When I took my first police job in 2012, I moved two hours away from my hometown. I moved into an apartment I couldn't afford in a new city where my coworkers were the only people I knew. By policy, officers weren't allowed to socialize with trainees, leaving me entirely alone on my off time.

I'm an avid Boston Bruins fan, but I couldn't afford cable in my apartment. I couldn't stream the games on my phone because the Wi-Fi I borrowed from the neighbor downstairs wasn't strong enough to handle the live feed.

I found an Irish pub just down the road from my apartment that played the Bruins games on the TVs over the bar. On nights I had off from work, I would take myself to the pub for dinner. I'd order a Coors Light and a plate of nachos and nurse both for as long as possible to watch the game.

The pub was downtown in a strip of shops they called the mall. It was a cute area, blocked off from traffic and bricked over for pedestrians with a fountain and a handful of benches.

There was a municipal lot nearby, and I would park my car and walk down the mall to the pub at game time. I didn't have a lot else going on at the time, so my Bruins ritual became somewhat of a routine.

Being young and having just recently moved away, I was often lonely and homesick during that time. Occasionally a friend would come and visit me, but most nights, I was alone. At least hanging out at the pub got me out of my apartment, and I was around other people. Best of all, I didn't have to miss out on my team's goals.

The bartender got to know me, if only by sight. A few other regulars would ask me how I was. Some other Bruins fans had grown accustomed to seeing me, and they might say hello when I came in. Occasionally, a guy might even try to flirt with me for a minute or two. Work and Bruins games at the pub were essentially all I had.

My FTO pulled me into the library of the police department one afternoon for a meeting. The library was really just a small conference room that happened to have a built-in bookshelf. No one used the library to read, and the shelves only housed out-of-date law books and some of the local high school's yearbooks. It seemed like the library's only real function was a forum for serious, closed-door conversations.

My FTO sat me down and told me I needed to stop going to The Cave. He told me that people had seen me there and informed me I was getting a bad reputation among other police officers.

To say I was confused would have been an understatement.

I had heard mentions of The Cave, a seedy bar where shady characters hung out, but I didn't even know where it was. I had certainly never been there, and I told my FTO this. He looked at me skeptically and told me how delicate my reputation was and how hard I needed to work to keep it intact.

It turns out, The Cave was also serviced by the municipal parking lot I had been using when I visited the Irish pub. Apparently, other officers had seen my car parked there and decided I must be up to no good in The Cave, thus starting a rumor and damaging the reputation I hadn't even established yet.

Mentally, I was crushed.

I couldn't fathom someone starting a rumor about me having never even met me. I had been on the job for only a few months, and the parking lot wasn't even in the town I worked in. This meant that it was officers from a different department that were spying on me, having never met me and likely only heard my name in relation to my hiring.

The pub had become a place to unwind mentally, but I no longer felt comfortable going there. I holed myself inside my apartment for months following that conversation.

I was afraid to go anywhere. I was worried someone might see me and think the wrong thing. The situation changed how I felt about the town and the area. I was so upset that I considered leaving and moving back home. It was a long, lonely winter.

Things got a little better when I was no longer on probation and I was allowed to socialize with my colleagues. I allowed myself to leave my apartment and started feeling less lonely. I developed friendships, and I eventually moved on from the original rumor.

But I never forgot the way that rumor started. Someone started talking about me just because they noticed my car in a parking lot. I knew that my job in law enforcement would put my actions under a microscope, but I hadn't expected to have to defend actions I hadn't even committed.

Throughout my career, there were plenty of other rumors. I was always having an affair with someone or sleeping with someone else. Most of the rumors weren't even that creative.

The outrageousness of the rumors sunk in after I changed departments. I started working in a neighboring city when I left my original department. I had only been there a few days and was still learning the ropes.

I was sitting at a computer in the patrol office when an officer I knew by sight but had never talked to stuck his head in the door.

"Hey," he said, introducing himself, "did you know we're fucking?"

I stared at him.

I had seen this officer maybe twice in my life before this moment. These were the first words we'd ever exchanged.

"Yeah," he said, with a casual shrug, "everyone at the such-and-such department is saying that's why you made the switch to this PD. Funny, right?" He laughed and walked away.

I had never even been in the same room with this officer before this moment, and people were talking about us sleeping together. How could that even make sense? I apparently found it less amusing than he did, as he was still laughing about it the next time I ran into him.

Then again, why shouldn't he find it funny? It didn't hurt his reputation at all if people thought we were having sex. He was allowed to have sex with anyone he wanted. Men always were. In fact, it turns out he was actually having sex with several people, but I was not one of them.

Once again, I found myself on the raw end of an utterly baseless rumor. It was ridiculous.

How could I be sleeping with a guy I'd literally never met? Maybe we were meeting up at the bar I'd never been to. Wouldn't that be a juicy story!

CHAPTER 19
INAPPROPRIATE BEHAVIOR

In addition to sleeping with everyone from all the surrounding police departments, I was also doing other terribly inappropriate things in my spare time.

Not long after I was off probation, I received a social media friend request from a woman I'd never met. I recognized her name and connected her as the wife of one of my coworkers. I thought nothing of accepting the friend request. I figured she was just trying to be nice. A few other wives had sent me friend requests, and I'd actually become friends with a few of them, so this didn't seem like that big of a deal.

A few days later, I was called into my sergeant's office. He shut the door and asked me to sit down. I'd never been in trouble before, but this sure felt like it would be the first time. I racked my brain, trying to think of something I had messed up, but I couldn't think of anything.

My sergeant informed me that a complaint had been filed against me. The woman who had sent me the friend request had contacted my sergeant and complained that there were inappropriate photos of me on my social media page. The photos she was referring to were of me wearing a bikini. The woman felt they were inappropriate and should be considered conduct unbecoming of an officer.

After getting access to my private social media account, this woman I had never met combed through my photos and located pictures of me she felt were too revealing. She filed a complaint with my sergeant because I was a twenty-something-year-old woman wearing a bathing suit.

To make matters worse, my sergeant had actually entertained the complaint.

He told me he had viewed the photos in question, and while he didn't think they were technically inappropriate, he advised me to be careful what I post on social media.

I asked him if I was allowed to post pictures on my private, personal account of me in a bathing suit. He assured me I was. He then said he just wanted me to be aware that people were watching me and making assumptions about me based on the things I post, so I might want to consider that when deciding what I did and didn't put on the Internet.

My mind was truly blown. I wasn't posting selfies of me in lingerie with racy captions. I was wearing a bikini. I was being lectured on social media etiquette by a man old enough to be my father because an insecure wife didn't want her husband working too closely with a young woman.

My social media accounts were already locked down to try to ensure as much privacy as possible, but I decided I didn't want to take any chances. I unfriended and blocked this particular woman just because I was especially mad at her, and then I deactivated all my accounts. I was disgusted at the thought of my normal, everyday life being used against me at work.

Before deactivating my accounts, I clicked on some of my coworkers' profiles. There were plenty of photos of them shirtless, pictures of them flexing at the gym, and photos of them drinking beers and goofing off. There were even photos of them with bikini-clad women.

The double standard was obvious. I was sure no one had ever combed through any of my coworkers' pages and complained about pictures of them. No one complained about them flaunting their chests or biceps. No one felt their behavior was unbecoming of an officer. None of that matters when you're a man.

It's only an issue if you're a woman.

CHAPTER 20
DIFFERENT PAY FOR THE SAME JOB

I'd always been told it's rude to talk about money and salaries with other people. You don't discuss what you or anyone else makes. Money is an uncomfortable topic for a lot of people to talk about. Some people even struggle to discuss it with their spouses. Perhaps we made it this way by believing lies like it's rude to talk about our salaries. Maybe if we didn't push this rumor, people wouldn't find money such a difficult topic to talk about.

Police salaries are public information. Members of the public are entitled to know the salaries of their local police officers. In the town I worked for, everyone's salaries were listed in the annual report. Somewhere in my brain, I knew this, but I had no reason to care what anyone else was making.

Our town operated on a step program. You started at a specific step, and each year you moved up. It was pretty simple and seemed foolproof. I understood how much I was making and that I would add to that number each year.

It didn't really matter to me what my coworkers were making because I didn't think it affected me. I never thought I had any reason to check the annual report to see anyone else's salaries, even though I had every right to do so. But money is weird and awkward, and as long as I knew how much money was going into my bank account every week, why should it matter to me how much was going into anyone else's?

When I was hired in September of 2012, I was 22 years old. I had a bachelor's degree in English and no real-world police experience. A month later, a second new recruit was hired. He didn't have a degree, nor did he have any relevant experience. We went through the academy together and returned to our department for our FTO programs. I technically outranked him, but only because I was hired first. Other than that one-month difference, we were on the same path.

Several years into our careers, we were standing together in the department's kitchen when he mentioned something about his pay. It was an off-hand comment, and at first, I didn't think anything of the numbers he'd mentioned because, again, I didn't care. I didn't go into law enforcement to get rich. I knew I wasn't going to make millions doing the job.

But it eventually struck me that this officer and I should be on the exact same step making the same amount of money. We essentially started together, and the only difference between us, other than our gender, was that I had a degree.

But he was making over fifty cents an hour more than I was.

Fifty cents doesn't seem like anything worth getting worked up about. I've found more change than that under the driver's seat of my car. But over the course of a year, that's more than a thousand dollars difference. And even if it wasn't, it's the principle of the thing!

A quick peek at the previous year's annual report revealed that every officer in the department was making more than me, even those who'd been hired after me with no experience. The only notable difference between myself and any of the others was that I was a female, and they were not.

After a few deep breaths and some time to calm down, I took my findings to the Human Resources department. I didn't come out and accuse them of paying me less than all my male coworkers, but I made a point to acknowledge that it was an awfully strange coincidence.

Of course, Human Resources investigated my claims and declared it a clerical error. They quickly moved my pay rate to align with the officer I was initially hired with.

They didn't offer to explain how this clerical error was made. They didn't offer to back pay me the difference for what I should have been making for years. They didn't even offer me an apology.

HR simply promised a mistake like that wouldn't happen again.

It's a crock of shit that you shouldn't talk about how much you make with other people. That's a lie put in place to ensure employees don't know the value of their work and don't know whether or not they're being mistreated.

Sure, it's partially my own fault because I had access to the annual report my entire career and never bothered to check it. Instead, I blindly - and naively - chose to assume my employer was taking care of me. I had access to the report, but so didn't everyone else. And it is, after all, their job to take care of these things.

Was it a mistake? A simple clerical error no one noticed? Who knows.

What I do know is that if my coworker hadn't been willing to talk about his salary, I might never have known I was being undervalued. If an employer tells you talking about your salary with other employees is not allowed, they're trying to hide something from you.

Employees shouldn't be worth more or less based on what may or may not be between their legs.

CHAPTER 21

GIRL PROBLEMS

I've openly talked about some of the chronic illnesses I suffer from, and one I talk about a lot is endometriosis. I've been struggling with endometriosis for most of my police career. If you're not aware, endometriosis is a painful disorder where the tissue that normally lines the walls of your uterus grows outside of it.

I deal with constant pelvic pain, debilitating cramps, and other issues in relation to this disorder. It was always incredibly painful to wear my duty belt during a flare. The weight and pressure would make me feel nauseous, and I'd be practically blind with pain.

None of my coworkers ever took me very seriously when I described this pain. They'd all been conditioned to believe period cramps were no big deal, and convincing them that endometriosis was anything other than a bad period was like talking to a wall. I shouldn't have had to try to explain my condition to my coworkers, but it felt important that I try.

Sometimes at the end of a shift, a coworker might catch me taking my gun belt off at the station to relieve the pain and pressure. I'd drape my belt over my lap while I typed up reports or lay it out on a nearby chair. I'd get teased about my inability to handle wearing my uniform for an entire shift. To avoid this, I tried taking time off during some of my more painful flares, but then I was criticized for using my sick days for "stupid" reasons.

Eventually, I tried to resolve the issue through surgery, hoping it would eliminate most of my pain. Unfortunately, the surgery only made things worse. I met with my chief and asked for more time off to recover. Since I'd just gone out for surgery to "resolve" the issue, he didn't understand why I needed more time off. It was difficult to explain to him what was happening in my body since he had no experience to relate it to.

Shortly after this conversation, the Town Administrator called me into his office. The Town Administrator and I rarely spoke. He was a frustrating, small-minded man with little understanding of how the town functioned and no idea how policing worked.

I was forced to sit in his office while he told me he fully understood my struggle because another town employee also suffers from endometriosis. He told me this employee, who had a desk job, was able to overcome her issues to be successful at work. He then started asking intrusive medical questions about what treatments I'd already tried for my pain. He then started trying to push acupuncture on me as a solution, citing ridiculous claims that it could cure me and offering to make me an appointment with a clinic he endorsed.

Feeling incredibly uncomfortable, I nodded until there was a break in the conversation where I could get up and leave. I had no desire to discuss the functioning of my uterus with the Town Administrator, nor did I want his medical advice. I felt violated by this man probing my medical history.

Despite ongoing pain, I was determined to return to police work. For the next several months, I endured appointment after appointment searching for a cure. I tried physical therapies, pain medications, pain therapy, and even hypnosis. Nothing helped my daily pain.

Finally, the difficult decision to perform a hysterectomy was made. I was only 31 years old at the time, and though I had no plans to have children, giving up the ability to potentially have children was incredibly difficult. To make matters worse, multiple doctors attempted to talk me out of the procedure, citing that my future husband might want children and that removing my uterus could be detrimental to his wishes. While medical sexism is a conversation for another day, to say I was frustrated is an understatement.

After my surgery, I felt like less of a woman. The irony was not lost on me that I had spent my entire career trying to diminish my femininity, and now I had given up my most feminine organ. I thought of the chief who'd told me I had plenty of time to get pregnant. I thought of all the times coworkers had made jokes about the fact that I might be pregnant because I wasn't feeling well. I thought of all the direct and indirect references made toward my body and its ability to carry a child.

There were a lot of emotions tied up in that surgery. After pathology, I learned that I'd also had adenomyosis in addition to endometriosis. Like endometriosis, adenomyosis has to do with the tissue that lines the uterus, but in this case, instead of growing outside of the uterus, it grows into the uterine walls. It's an extremely painful condition, but unlike endometriosis, it can be cured. Removing the uterus removed the adenomyosis. At least I was finally rid of one source of pain.

Recovering from a hysterectomy is difficult, both mentally and physically. My body ached, and it was difficult to move. I struggled to work out, and my fitness level declined. As my fitness level declined, so did my mental health. I was frustrated with the amount of pain I was still dealing with daily, but I also struggled with the mental repercussions of losing my uterus. It sounds silly, but it's sort of like mourning the loss of a child you'll never have.

When I was away from my department, not one of my coworkers reached out to me to see how I was doing. No one checked in on me or sent me a text. It was like they'd forgotten all about me while I was gone.

I learned later that they hadn't forgotten about me. They were just busy making fun of me. Apparently, they thought it was funny that I couldn't handle my "period cramps" and blamed my low pain tolerance for scheduling difficulties.

After months of physical therapy and pain management, I was ready to return to patrol work. My chief asked me to get a letter from my doctor clearing me to return full-time. This seemed reasonable since I'd taken my leave of absence based on a medical issue.

I returned a few days after my yearly physical with a doctor's note clearing me to return to work. The chief told me the town needed me to see the occupational doctor to be cleared. The Town Administrator wanted an unbiased, third-party opinion that I was fit for duty.

This felt biased, especially as the Town Administrator was aware of some of my medical history. It felt like he was looking for a reason to deny my return. I tried to argue that I already had a doctor's note clearing me to return, but it didn't appear that this was an argument I would win.

Begrudgingly, I went to the appointment. I was once again cleared to return to work without issue. The Town Administrator received a letter from the occupational doctor clearing me for duty. He had expected a copy of my medical records to accompany this letter. When he wasn't sent a copy of my file, he called the doctor's office and tried to obtain one. That's a HIPPA violation no doctor's office would ever touch, but that didn't deter the Town Administrator.

He then called my Primary Care doctor, wanting to discuss my health with her. When this was also shot down, he drafted language for a new doctor's note he wanted to be signed by my doctor.

Meanwhile, I was already back at work. I'd returned after the occupational doctor had cleared me, and I was unaware of the Town Administrator attempting to violate my rights. I didn't find out there was a problem until the first payday rolled around, and I was told the Town Administrator was withholding my paycheck until he got the copy of the specific doctor's note he wanted.

I was outraged. Not only was it federally illegal for the town to withhold my paycheck, but I'd already returned to work. As far as I was concerned, I'd already been cleared twice by two different doctors, and I was good to go.

I had jumped through every hoop the Town had required, and still, they weren't happy. It wasn't lost on me that I was the only female employee and that none of my male coworkers had ever been required to go to such extremes to return to work after an injury. I was still furious.

Would so much effort have been put into clearing me for duty if I'd had knee surgery? It seems unlikely. But knee surgery can happen to anyone. Only those with female organs can have a hysterectomy.

CHAPTER 22
PET PEEVES

All jobs have annoying aspects. For every ten things I loved about law enforcement, there was something that simply annoyed me no matter what. Some of those things were function-related, like having to do repetitive paperwork or fill in archaic forms that could easily be digitalized and condensed. Those were the kinds of annoyances I simply rolled my eyes at.

During my career, however, I developed pet peeves that had nothing to do with the function of the job and everything to do with my place in it. I grew to hate the smart-ass comments, like "I'd let you handcuff me!" or "do you take your handcuffs home at night?" I hated when people would tell me how I looked in uniform. I hated being objectified.

My biggest pet peeve was the way no one seemed to notice the little ways sexism manifested itself in the job

I was constantly being fit into roles specifically because I was a woman. Traditional gender roles, rather than talent, skill, or interest, seemed to play a large part in the roles I was assigned. Several times when I asked why I had been tasked with certain obviously gendered things, my supervisor would seem baffled. "Who else would be capable of doing it?" I quickly learned this was not a compliment to my abilities but simply an acknowledgment of my lack of male genitalia.

It was automatically assumed that I would be involved with children's programs and community outreach because I was a woman. I was volunteered to participate in collaboration with the Special Olympics because I was a woman. There were all these assumptions made about me that had nothing to do with my likes and dislikes and everything to do with the fact that I did not have a penis.

It's frustrating because I do enjoy being involved in children's programming and participating in the Special Olympics. I had fun representing the police department at specific community events, and I would have volunteered to fill many of these roles had it been an option. My annoyance came from the fact that it wasn't an option. It was an assumption.

Of course, I was equally peeved when someone assumed I couldn't do something or didn't know how to do something because of my gender. If I had a dollar for every time someone man-splained to me how to clean my duty weapon, I probably wouldn't have to worry about retirement.

Once, while carrying a sandwich board sign advertising a community event I had been designated to organize, my chief asked me three times if I could "manage" the sign. The sign probably weighed less than the bulletproof vest I was wearing.

These assumptions are simply manifestations of sexism. You're assuming that because of my gender, I can't do something. You're solely focusing on my gender rather than my capabilities or strengths. There's a difference between offering to be helpful and making a blanket assumption of inability.

For instance, if the chief had asked if I needed help with the sign or asked if there was anything else that needed to be carried over, that would have been generous and helpful. But specifically asking if I felt I was capable of managing it made it clear that he wasn't offering to be helpful, but offering because he felt I was not capable.

I also absolutely hated when I accidentally fit into a gendered stereotype, opening the door for people to people justified in their sexism.

One of my departments had a radar trailer, and I sucked at backing it up. I did not suck at this task because I'm a woman. I sucked at this task because the radar trailer was a pain in the ass. Lots of people had a hard time with it. But every time I struggled with it, jokes would be made about women and their universal inability to back a trailer up.

I'm also bad at math. Again, not because I'm a woman, but because I am very much a right-brain thinker. Even though there are plenty of men who are bad at math, when I would get caught using my fingers to figure out how many miles over the speed limit someone was going, it was because I was a woman.

I know that these aren't examples of outrageous acts of sexism, but they are constant small reminders that it exists. Not every act of sexism is overt and over the top. Some, like these, are simply small reminders that the people around you think less of you based on a biological fact beyond your control.

CHAPTER 23
NO SUCH THING AS SEXISM

A fellow officer once told me there was no such thing as sexism in police work. He acknowledged that there probably used to be sexism in police work "way back when," but he was confident it no longer existed.

I lost a lot of respect for him that day.

We were sitting together in a slow moment, chatting about god knows what, when I decided to vent a little about a sexist comment a guy had made to me during a traffic stop. I wasn't necessarily angry about the comment. I was just looking for a little sympathy from my counterpart. I probably would have been more than satisfied if my coworker had responded with, "what a dick," and then moved on.

But instead of sympathy, my coworker told me I was overreacting.

He told me he had never seen anyone be truly sexist in his years of law enforcement. I told him that given his gender, it seemed unlikely he'd have directly experienced sexism, but that if he hadn't seen sexism directed at me on calls we'd worked together, he hadn't been paying close attention.

My coworker assured me he would have noticed if someone had "actually" been sexist toward me and that he was positive sexism no longer existed in police work.

"Everyone treats cops with the same amount of respect," he said, "if they're being an asshole to you, it's because they don't like cops, not because they're sexist."

I agreed that there are certainly individuals who don't like the police in general and are disrespectful to all officers for that reason, regardless of gender. But I did not agree that all people treated all police officers with the exact same amount of respect.

I tried to further explain my point by drawing his attention to a call we had just recently responded to together. In that instance, a man was causing a disturbance at a local laundromat. He was using the location as a warm hangout on a cold day, but he had overstayed his welcome. He was scaring customers and getting unruly with the management staff. They wanted him removed from the premises and asked him not to return.

The call itself was fairly straightforward. I arrived on scene first and began trying to speak with the individual. He was unhappy to see me, to say the least. He kept calling me a bitch and telling me to mind my own business. I was calmly explaining his options to him when the other officer arrived.

Once he walked in, the individual in question refused to speak to me. He directed all his comments toward the male officer and refused to acknowledge anything I said or asked. He kept telling the male officer that he didn't trust "bitches in power," stating that he was a

Veteran and knew from experience that women in uniform were "up to no good."

My coworker seemed to remember the altercation differently than I did. "That wasn't sexist. He just didn't like you."

"He didn't like me because I'm a woman," I argued.

"Yeah, but that doesn't mean he's sexist," he said, rolling his eyes at me.

I felt like screaming, "THAT'S EXACTLY WHAT IT MEANS," but I tried to remain calm. I pointed out a few other examples from other calls we'd worked together, hoping he might be smart enough to realize his own ignorance.

Spoiler alert: he was not.

"None of that is any different than when I show up on a call, and someone calls me an asshole," he said. "It's just part of the job. We all deal with it."

I think I was in actual shock while I tried to digest this comment. My esteemed colleague went on to explain that part of the issue was the fact that I was trying to make it about gender when gender had nothing to do with it at all, an issue he told me women seem to be prone to.

He finished his enlightened speech by telling me I was being too sensitive.

He may have had more to say on the subject, but this is the point I drove away from him. I was disgusted by his inability to recognize blatant examples of sexism that happened right in front of him, and he had the nerve to tell me I was overreacting. I was enraged that he felt entitled to mansplain my own experiences to me.

I was also upset that a fellow officer could be so closed-minded.

I've never been able to look at him the same way.

In my mind, it's one thing to recognize the sexism happening around you and not care, but to deny its existence altogether? It would seem to me that the only way someone could be so blind as to feel that sexism doesn't exist is if he believes the sexism is justified.

CHAPTER 24
THE CULTURE PROBLEM

Whenever the topic of sexual harassment comes up in conversations, guys will jump to tell you that they're not part of the problem.

"I'm not one of those guys who would ever sexually harass a coworker," they'll exclaim with shocked looks on their faces as if the very thought has put a vial taste in their mouths.

These types of guys will usually follow up this statement by saying, "I just think if women are going to be in law enforcement, they should understand the culture!"

Everything always comes back to the culture of police work. It's not sexual harassment, sexism, or discrimination! It's just the culture!

I've heard this phrase so many times throughout my career. Everyone is so quick to blame the culture as if it's some autonomous being that we're incapable of controlling. Who do these guys think created this culture? Who do they think continues to cultivate it?

As with any culture, it's a learned process. No one is born with a cultural understanding. It's taught by superiors and developed through experience. In any form, the culture is created by the people.

Police work is no different. It's a culture developed by men and has continued to be cultivated by them. They pass down the unspoken rules, the values, and the biases to each new generation stepping out of the academy. The culture of police work exists because of police officers.

Blaming the culture for sexism and sexual harassment is probably as close as we're going to get to men actually taking responsibility for the problem.

Before anyone has a coronary, we can address the whole "not all men" issue. Yes, there are male officers who don't outwardly engage in making sexual or sexist comments. I've had many coworkers over the years who never came close to crossing that line. However, those same coworkers stood by while others made those comments. Those coworkers didn't speak up when sexist comments were made. Those coworkers, as nice as they were, did nothing to change the culture.

This is a cultural problem. Women can't change this culture alone. In fact, I'd argue we can't change the culture at all.

As a woman, I can point out the flaws, but I'll be labeled whinny. I can scream and yell about the injustices all day long, but I'll be labeled "too sensitive." I can push back and fight tooth and nail to make these points, but at the end of the day, all I'll ever be is a woman complaining about "the way things are in a male-dominated space."

The only way to change the culture is for the men in that male-dominated space to recognize that they're the problem. The men have to look around and recognize that they've created this environment that forces women to endure the sexism and sexual harassment in order to be accepted. They have to be willing to admit that that isn't right, and then they have to be willing to make changes.

Until that day, law enforcement, like so many other male-dominated careers, will remain a boys club. It will never be a place for women to be themselves. Women will continue to have to create personas that allow them to be one of the guys instead of simply being who she is.

Until we change the culture, law enforcement will never be anything other than male-dominated.

About The Author

Nenia Corcoran attended the New Hampshire Police Academy in 2012 as a member of the 160th Academy Class. She served as a patrol officer for three different departments in the Upper Valley of New Hampshire.

She was named to the Central New Hampshire Special Operations Unit in 2016, and at the time, she was the only active female SWAT operator in the state.

In 2007, I graduated from North Reading High School and branched out into a world beyond my small town. After high school, I completed an undergraduate degree and two master's programs. In addition to all that, I also graduated from the New Hampshire Police Academy. I consider myself to be a highly educated and very knowledgeable woman.

Despite all that education, there are hundreds of lessons I still had to learn the hard way. Thousands of times I had to ask myself why no one ever told me about x, y or z. Why did I spend hundreds of thousands of dollars on an education that barely prepared me for life in the real world?

The reality is, there are multiple forms of education. Formal education is generally thought of as taking place in a structured school setting, involving designated teachers and lesson plans. But this only accounts for a fraction of the education that each person receives throughout their lives.

We find "informal" education in the form of books, TV, the internet, other people and our own experiences. The truth is, the majority of our education comes from this informal education. If we pay attention, we can find education in nearly every situation. As we navigate our daily lives, we learn more and more about the world around us. Sometimes those lessons are good, other times those lesson make us question everything we know about humanity. Each lesson is another grade in our life-long education.

Anyone can become a teacher, even when you least expect it. One thing I've learned (consider this your first tip!) is to never underestimate someone's ability to teach you something. Some of the most insightful words of wisdom I've ever heard have come out of the mouths of children under ten. I learned a lot about true love from a woman with dementia and the definition of happiness from a young man with down syndrome. Anyone, at anytime, can be a teacher.

As I thought about all the things I've learned over the years, I realized that most of the really important things came to me outside of the classroom. While I am very proud of the extremely expensive pieces of paper that hang on the wall of my bedroom collecting dust, I know that they don't really represent how much I know about the world.

In fact, if I'm being completely honest, my degrees don't really mean all that much at all. Sure, they look nice on my resume and I get to brag about them on my LinkedIn page, but at the end of the day, they're a very small piece of who I am.

As it turns out, they're almost irrelevant to the work I do every day. They didn't make me a better police officer. No one treats me differently because I have them, and despite popular belief, I don't make any more money because of them. They are simply boxes that I checked off on my own bucket list. An accomplishment my mother could brag to her friends about, but nothing more.

That leads me to the very first thing I didn't learn in school. No one ever told me it was okay to not go the traditional four-year college route. When I was a junior at North Reading High School, I believed that if I didn't get into a decent four-year college and graduate with at least an undergraduate degree, I would be considered a failure.

The options that were presented to me by my teachers and my guidance counselor appeared to be: serve your country in the military or get a bachelor's degree. That was it. There was no mention of tech-schools, no talk of certification programs, nothing. I was convinced that the only way to make yourself successful was by following the traditional path toward a college or university. Degrees were the path to success. The way it seemed, without a degree, you might as well plan to be homeless.

Turns out, this is not the case at all. Want to know what a degree gets you? Debt. I have more student loan debt than I'll probably ever be able to pay. I financed three degrees and a graduate certificate. I'll still be paying off my student loans when my own kids get to college. At the time, I thought that was just what you had to do. It was the sacrifice you had to make in order to become successful, because you absolutely had to get the degree.

Do I regret getting my degrees? No, because I'm the type of person who really enjoys "formal" education. I love class discussions on literary theories and symbolism and arguing that one opinion is better than another. I truly enjoyed taking my classes. If money wasn't an object, I'd take more classes just to take them. But I know classes aren't for everyone.

There are other options out there besides traditional colleges, and you can become just as successful (if not more successful) by pursuing some of those paths. If you're the type of person that doesn't like school, I encourage you to take a look at all the other paths you can take after leaving high school. There is no best way to enter "the real world."

However you choose to do it is going to be just fine.

MONEY

In all my years of formal education, no one ever talked to me about money.

In fact, money was sort of an abstract concept when I was growing up. I knew I needed it in order to provide for myself, but I didn't really understand how I was going to get it or how I was going to take care of it. I also didn't understand that it can very easily take over your entire life.

It's easy to ignore the importance of money when someone else is providing for you. I was lucky enough to grow up in an upper-middle class family. We weren't rich, but I never worried about where my next meal was coming from and I rarely wanted for anything I didn't eventually receive. While my parents made me "work" for the things like a laptop or a cellphone, I'm sure I never truly earned the gifts I was given.

It wasn't until I was living alone in an apartment trying to support myself with my first real job that I learned how quickly money can become the focus of your anxiety, and how hard it is to break free from a downward spiral once you've started in that direction.

While on paper, my paycheck should have more than covered my rent, I quickly learned that reality is a lot messier than just making a budget. I had grossly underestimated my monthly budget for things like gas and food, and quickly found out that my pay periods didn't perfectly align with my bills. To fill the gaps, I started putting charges on my credit card. It didn't take long before I added a hefty amount of credit card debt to my mounting student loan debt.

To make matters worse, I never learned how to properly file my taxes. A missing deduction led to the IRS coming after me for $1,200 I certainly didn't have. I was drowning, and I had no idea how to save myself. The worst part was, I didn't have any idea how I had gotten to this point. I had a good job that paid me well, so I assumed that everything would be fine.

Unfortunately, having a decent job is only a fraction of the equation. Money stress is a huge factor in our society. Stressing over finances has led to divorces, health issues and even deaths. It's a very real problem. So why don't we talk about it?

Money is probably one of the fundamental factors of our society. Everyone has a basic understanding of the fact that without money, you can't make it very far. In America, the idea of having money is linked to the feeling of safety, security and comfort. Nearly every aspect of our lives is controlled in some way by money.

I hear a lot of talk about teaching our kids the value of money, and I am 100% on board with that. However, we need to teach more than just the value of money. We need to talk about taxes and debt and investing and budgeting. We need to teach them how money factors into life and how to handle it. We need to teach kids from a very young age how to actually deal with money, not just it's value.

I won't pretend that this section is going to help you better manage your money. In fact, I'll be blunt and tell you it won't. I am not claiming to be a financial guru who can tell you exactly what to do with your money in order to be successful. In fact, if I'm being honest I still don't know what to do with my money in order to be successful. If you happen to figure it out, feel free to let me know, I'm open for suggestions.

I am a 30-something year old, well educated woman who has no idea how to manage her student loan debt. I don't know how to invest in the stock market, nor do I have any idea whether you should open a ROTH or an IRA. I actually don't even know what either of those two things are, I just heard them on a Fidelity commercial.

But this is exactly my point. Why don't I know those things? Why wasn't there some class along the way where someone explained how to be an adult with your money. We all eventually get to this point, so shouldn't someone start talking to us about it before we dig ourselves $100,000 in the hole?

There are a few things I can tell you about money that I didn't learn from school.

I learned very quickly that credit cards are not free money. I was barely out of high school when I got the first letter telling me I had been pre-approved for some ridiculous spending limit on a credit card. Interest rates meant nothing to me, I bet I didn't even look to see if the card had an annual fee.

It was so easy to swipe the card and use the fake money to buy the things I wanted. I could have everything I wanted without touching the money in my bank account. I thought it was perfect.

Except that isn't how credit cards work. You might pay up front with your fake money, but you need real money to pay off the card. When you only put a little real money toward your credit card balance, you start racking up interest. Turns out, the interest is pretty important to pay attention to. It adds up quick and starts increasing the amount of money you actually owe. It deepens the spiral and makes it much harder to get out once you're headed down.

Once you're in the situation where your money is causing you stress, it can quickly become overwhelming.

Money became all I was ever thinking about.

How could I make more?

What did I need to pay first?

Was I missing a payment?

Which payments should I make when?

I started losing sleep, which caused me to get run down, which caused me to get sick, which caused me to miss work. See where I'm going with this? It was not ideal. They say money can't buy happiness, but not having money was making me pretty unhappy.

Digging out of that hole took a lot of work, a little help and some luck, too. I was able to find an apartment for much cheaper than the one I had been living in. I was able to rework my budget and get out from under my credit card debt. I still have a crushing amount of student loans, but I'm working on those, too. I was lucky enough to get a (nearly) fresh start, but there's a lot of things I could have done to avoid almost going bankrupt. I learned these lessons the hard way, but I'd rather you learn them from me so you don't have to experience them yourself!

There's no reason to be in a rush to move out of your parent's house. If you're living somewhere rent free, soak that shit up. Seriously! You might think it's embarrassing to say you're living in your parent's basement, but every extra month you stay in that environment is money in your pocket. Obviously, there are situations and circumstances where this theory doesn't work, but give it some serious consideration if it's an option for you. There is no shame in saving money.

I was in a huge rush to move out of my parent's house, where I was living rent free, not paying for utilities or for food. One of my biggest regrets is moving out too early. I moved out because I wanted my "freedom" and "independence," but I would have been able to afford a lot more of that if I had stuck it out a little bit longer. A friend of mine lived with his mom until he was 26. He paid off all his student loans, owns his truck outright and just put a large down payment on a home of his own. There's probably someone who laughed at him at some point for living with his mom, but I'm pretty sure he's getting the last laugh now.

On the flip side of the coin (yes, this pun was absolutely intended), money shouldn't be your single motivator. I know this is going to sound contradicting to everything I just said, but sometimes money isn't everything. Yes, you need money to survive. Finances does have to be taken into account, but there are actually somethings that money can't buy.

I took a pay cut in order to be happy.

I was working in a very negative environment. The employees weren't appreciated, and everyone was unhappy. The environment was toxic. I could actually feel myself get angry when I walked through the doors. However, the job paid significantly better than any others in the area.

After months of negativity and feeling my mental health decline, I decided that the extra few dollars an hour wasn't worth my sanity. I took the pay cut to move to a better environment, and I've never regretted that.

The money was good, but feeling good when I walked into work every day was better. Society makes it sound like you always need to be looking for the next promotion, the next chance to move up, the next chance to make more money. Sometimes, especially when it comes to your career, there are benefits to weigh that don't have anything to do with cash.

Money shouldn't define you. Unless you move off the grid and start a homestead, money is going to play a big part in the rest of your life. It will likely determine where you live, what you drive and the type of clothes you wear. It will be a deciding factor in many of you bigger life decisions, but there are times it should have no place at all in your decision making.

It should never matter in a relationship. Money should never be used to hold a relationship together, nor should it be the reason one falls apart. It should never be held over one partner's head that they make more or less than the other. Money shouldn't be used to bribe or force a partner to stay or do anything he or she doesn't want to do. We'll talk a lot more about relationships later, but this warrants repeating.

Relationships should always be about more than money.

Your self-worth is also not defined by the dollar amount in your bank account. You don't matter less or more based on the amount of money in your wallet. You shouldn't associate how valuable you are as a person with the value in your account.

Money is a necessary evil. We need money to function, but we can't let money become the only reason we get up every day. You need to find a balance.

Remember that money is a stressor, so take the time to learn good money habits to eliminate some of that potential stress. When you do get to the point of pairing your finances with someone else's, be open and honest about them. Talk openly about money issues, and never blame them on one person or another. Try to keep money as a very small focus of your relationship, because your relationship should be built on a much stronger foundation than your bank account.

www.ingramcontent.com/pod-product-compliance
Lightning Source LLC
Chambersburg PA
CBHW022049020426
42335CB00012B/616